The Paintbrush

*A Magical Journey of Transformation
to Inspire Inner Peace and Enlightened Love*

TIA CRYSTAL

Copyright © 2022 by Tia Crystal

All rights reserved. No part of this book may be reproduced by any mechanical, photographic, or electronic process or in the form of a phonographic recording; nor may it be stored in a retrieval information system now known or hereafter invented, transmitted, or otherwise be copied for public or private use—other than for "fair use" as brief quotations embodied in critical articles and reviews—without written permission of the publisher.

Published by Quantum Shift Publishing

Editing, interior, and cover design by Quantum Shift Media
Cover art by Tia Crystal

Author coaching and editing by Joanna Infeld of Kora Press and Keren Kilgore of Quantum Shift Media

ISBN: 979-8-218-00821-5 Paperback
ISBN: 979-8-218-00822-2 eBook
Library of Congress Control Number: 2022909871

Denver, Colorado
QuantumShiftMedia.com

Dedication

This book is dedicated to my amazing children: Melissa, James, and Joshua.

To my parents, siblings, family, friends, teachers, and all the people with whom I have connected. With gratitude for the desire to search within and the awareness that we are more powerful than we know, I give thanks to the message and the messengers who showed me the way and gave me the chance to believe in myself.

Most of all, I want to thank the father of my children who allowed me to find my power. I dedicate this book to you, Jonathan.

Jonathan Mendel
1965-2020

*Everyone you meet is fighting a battle you
know nothing about. Be kind. Always.*
~Robin Williams

Accolades

Tia's Big Heart

You have Tia Crystal's life story in your hands! Well done. You have activated magic in your life. Tia will take you on a journey, and as you read her fascinating story, you will find yourself (just as I did) going deep inside to your own magical place.

When the student is ready, the teacher appears. I am glad you are here. Led by an angel at the age of 40, Tia set out to find her life's purpose. She left behind everything she was and, for a period of time, everything she knew. What was revealed to her will fascinate you, just as it did me when I first heard her story. I was wide-eyed with wonder as she told me about her courageous pilgrimage to Assisi.

In the many years I have known and loved Tia she has shared more pieces of her story with me. I sat rapt each time as I realized she really does live a rather magical life. She is a true teacher, not only talking the talk but, as you will read, walking it too. She has been led by a force, inspired by an angelic team, and has a deep sense of trust. She was able to follow her heart. As you read more about her incredible journey through life, you will find yourself

The Paintbrush

amused, amazed, and delighted to have found your way to this profound book.

Tia's magic shows up in her paintings, most of which sparkle with crystals and come alive with reflected light. It shows in her mindful teachings and meditations which take me to beautiful expansive places and shift my state of mind. It shows in the caring attention she gives to her family and her many friends.

For my last big birthday, Tia showed up with the most extraordinary cake I had ever seen. It had chocolate ganache on the inside, covered in fondant icing with a Tia Crystal masterpiece painted on top of the cake! A most delicious way to show love for a friend. Whatever Tia does, she does well and with style.

When I first got to really know Tia, she was recovering from a heartbreak. Here was a beautiful, kind, and gentle woman who was hurting big. She was vulnerable and open. As time went on, I could see that the heartbreak was a necessary part of her growth. As she gave herself over to her own healing process, she sparked a light inside her that took hold as a creative fire, one that burns still, carefully tended by her self-love.

As you get to know Tia through this extraordinary pilgrimage, you will find your heart opening. You will be able to feel her courage, her strength, her inspiration, and most important of all, her big love. Welcome to the magical life of Tia Crystal.

JoAnna Brandi
Author, Speaker, Consultant, Happiness Coach
January 2022

Tia the Magic Maker

Have you ever met someone you loved to be with? Someone who sizzled with enthusiasm and a deep desire to make the world brighter and better? Every time I have been with Tia Crystal, mostly professionally, and recently personally, this is how I have felt.

Albert Einstein asked a fundamental question for us all: "Is it a friendly universe?" Some people feel so much hurt, sadness, loss, or pain, that they cannot see their way to believe that there is a mysterious force at play and that everything happens for our benefit. Hence, they do not feel it is a friendly universe. If you believe it is friendly, you know that whatever is happening is happening for you and not against you, and it is all happening for a reason.

Tia makes life meaningful. She makes hearts smile. She understands that we suffer but does not dwell on the suffering. She wears the proverbial rose-colored glasses because she knows that is the way life is meant to be seen. From difficult, painful times to magical times, I have watched for over 15 years as Tia has improved her skill sets and utilized her talents to bring positive messages to all she meets. Her art, jewelry designs, and the enlightening character E Me Uni she created are merely the expressions of her soul's desire to paint the world with love and harmony.

One day you might meet her and revel in the beauty of her smile, her giggles, or her profound connection to spirit. I love being in her presence and learning from Tia to trust the process and welcome change.

The Paintbrush

You might only meet her through the words in this book. Consider that a blessing. I know she will show you how to communicate with love, kindness, and compassion.

May your life be magical, may the lenses you wear help you see the best life has to offer, and may you choose to color your world in love and feel that life is meant for you to thrive.

Thank you, Tia, for being the brightest light in our little universe and for inspiring the adults of tomorrow.

Liz Sterling
Author, Coach, Teacher, Motivational Speaker
January 2022

Tia the Energy Lady

In a time when I felt empty and was looking for guidance in my spiritual practice, I met Tia. I had no idea where to start or how to discover how to connect with spirit. Tia became my guru. She cracked me open at my core and lit a fire in my soul. She has guided me through transformation, disbelief, and uncertainty all the way to being so confidently connected to spirit that I am beginning to develop psychic skills. I never would have believed that I could have such a deep connection to a higher power if it hadn't been for the divine intervention initiated by my meeting Tia.

Being in Tia's presence sparks awe. There is something inherently different about her. She has beauty and grace, and something so much deeper—a celestial love pours out of her. When in her aura a person can feel it with every ounce of their being. She is like a goddess mother on a higher mission to support humanity's awakening.

Tia is one of the most inspiring people I have ever met. Her energy is contagious and when I am around her, I feel as if I am in the presence of someone other-worldly. She allows her inner child and her creativity to guide her discovery process. Tia pushes fear aside and instead leans into the wonder of possibility.

I am so happy that you will meet her through the pages of this book. She has been a profound catalyst for transformation in my life, and I know she has the ability to change the whole world. I am grateful to have met her again in this lifetime, and you will be, too.

Kendra McCarrick Beavis
Founder and CEO of the Brand Strategy Studio,
MOKA Creative
January 2022

Soul Sisters

Darling Tia,

We have been together for so… many years. Meeting you was very profound. From the moment we met, it felt as if we were looking into a mirror, seeing each other's souls. There is so much love and trust between us that no human could ever separate us.

Life has given us many challenges, but we have always turned darkness into light. I was probably the one that showed you your first spiritual ideas, but so quickly you understood and took a great leap of faith.

Over the last 28 years, I have watched you transform into an amazing confident woman... Teacher... Artist... so much more. Having you in my life is like a beautiful gemstone that I will treasure forever.

Keep on growing; the world needs people like you to shine your light and spread happiness into people's lives.

Forever your soul sister,
Marisol
2022

Contents

Dedication 3
Accolades. 5
    Tia's Big Heart 5
    Tia The Magic Maker 7
    Tia the Energy Lady. 8
    Soul Sisters 9
Introduction 17
    It's All About the Journey 17

Live ♥

Chapter 1: The Beginning 23
    My Protectors. 23
    World of Imagination 24
    Safe to Ask Why. 26
    Forming Belief Patterns 28

The Paintbrush

Chapter 2: The Wheels of Life Roll 33
    Dyslexia in 1968 34
    Convent, Hebrew School & Shopping 37
    The Sound of My Inner Voice 39
    You're Too Soft, Toughen Up! 39
    Blessed by the Pope 40
    Saved by Angels 41
    Report Card Mishaps 42
    Empath & Illusions 43
    Self-Bullying 45

Chapter 3: Please, Someone, Show Me the Way! 51
    Goodbye School 51
    #1 Hairstylist 52
    The Nut House 53
    Power of the Ego 55

Chapter 4: Motherhood and the Will to Live 59
    My First Marriage 59
    Trauma Begins 60
    Life or Death 62
    Where There Is a Will 65
    Mother Bear 66
    Healing the Trauma 67
    My Knight in Shining Armor 68

Contents

Love 💗

Chapter 5: Growing into Me 75
    Octopus SuperMum. 75
    Time for Me to Meet Tia 77
    Spiritual Seance 78
    White Cloud 80
    Mediumship Mentoring. 83
    Interior Designers to Ya-Ya Sisters 84
    Precious Souls. 84
    Sharing the Gifts with My Family 85
    Meeting Mother Meera 86
    What is Darshan 87
    Tia - Maria Girls in Madrid 88
    Train to Toledo You Hope! 89
    Attracting Goodness. 91
    Angels Around Me 93
    Learning to Have Faith and Trust 94

Chapter 6: Time to Be Broken Open 99
    The Tide Turned 99
    Someone Show Me the Way. 99
    The Messenger & the Message. 100
    Taking One Step at a Time 102

The Paintbrush

Train to Assisi 104
Happy Trekking 106
Courage to Face Your Fears 108

Enlightened

Chapter 7: Roses and Love 115
    The Attic Bedroom 115
    Child of the Rose 117
    Kaboom Assisi, Kaboom Tia 120
    Three Layers to Enlightened Love 121
    Me, Layer One 123
Chapter 8: Traumas Be Gone 129
    Layers of Stuck Trauma 129
    Void of Energy 130
    Easy Does It 133
Chapter 9: T For Tau 137
    Hello Morning, My Dear Friend 137
    Empathic Soul Energy Vampire 138
    Peace and Enlightened Love 141
Chapter 10: Time to Leave the Walls 153
    Father Mother Energy 153
    Italian Retail Therapy 155

Contents

    Hermitage of Carcieri 156
    To the Countryside, I Go 157
Chapter 11: The Paintbrush 163
    Halo of Roses 163
    Message Under a Bush 165
    Getting My Doodle On 167
    A Giggle Along the Way 169
    The Religion of Enlightened Love 170
Chapter 12: Saint Clare 177
    Alive With Light 178
    My Panties and Me 181
    Love From Us All 182
    Artist of Assisi 183
    Until We Meet Again, ... 186
Chapter 13: Birthing My Art 191
An Inspiring Message from Tia's Children 197
About the Author 201
    Award-Winning Artist 202
    Masterful Storyteller 204
    Public Speaker 205
    Best-Selling Author 205
    Contact Tia Crystal 205

Introduction

It's All About the Journey

What if all you needed every day was a paintbrush, some paint, and the world as your canvas in order to create your life the way you want it to be? In today's world, people search for answers outside of themselves. They look for external substances—drugs, alcohol, mindless entertainment—to enhance, dull, or drown out the emotions of stress, fear, and anxiety. Yet, the awareness and understanding that we seek are always within us.

Do you know how to access this powerful knowledge? Not by changing who you are but by changing how you love yourself. The key is treating yourself with tenderness, appreciation, love, and gratitude.

You are not what you have been programmed to believe you are. You are not the sum of other people's ideas or expectations about who you should be. You are not here simply to struggle through each day or just get by.

You are here for a reason—to live a big miracle every single day of your life.

Does that sound preposterous? It might be because most people have been conditioned to see their lives as a series of wishes, hopes, and dreams that are impossible to achieve.

The Paintbrush

Living a miracle is everyone's birthright. A miracle is what we are all here to experience, and it begins when we are born. But unfortunately, the mind is often caught up in a muddled web of confusing stories we have been fed by our parents, friends, teachers, and the media.

Who are you? What is your passion? What do you love? These simple questions may be hard to answer with complete, authentic truth if you have spent your whole life letting other people define you. Maybe you have become completely blinded to your own uniqueness, deaf to your inner voice.

Through this book, we will go on a journey of self-discovery together. My hope and wish are for you to see yourself through your own authentic heart, releasing out-of-date voices that long ago took up residence inside your head. This journey, I hope, will give you the gift and blessing of self-love that will shine a light on you—a jewel that is priceless, perfect, ageless, rare, and exquisite! When you find the genuine, authentic you, you will never again search for anything outside yourself. You will be so comfortable with who you are that you will shine as bright as the rarest jewel for all the world to see.

Are you ready to take a leap of faith with me? It will be *out there* at times, all the way into the mystic.

If I hadn't experienced what I am about to share with you myself, I would say, "This British lady is off her trolley," or even better, "She is barking mad!" When our journey together is finished, I think you will agree that being "off your trolley" is a thousand times better than being on a trolley, trudging through life without having an inkling of the magic inside of you.

I invite you to open the door to your own inner wisdom and join me on a journey of healing and transformation into a world of inner peace and enlightened love.

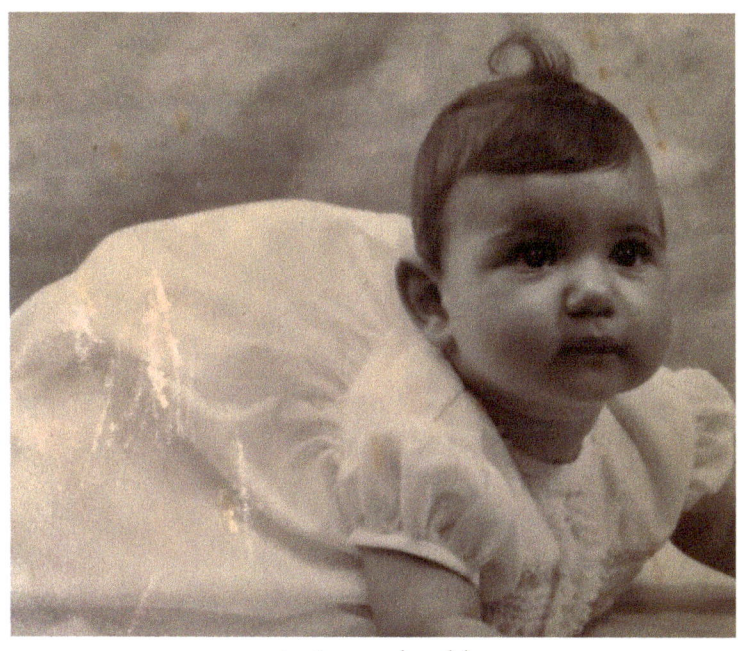

At 3 months old

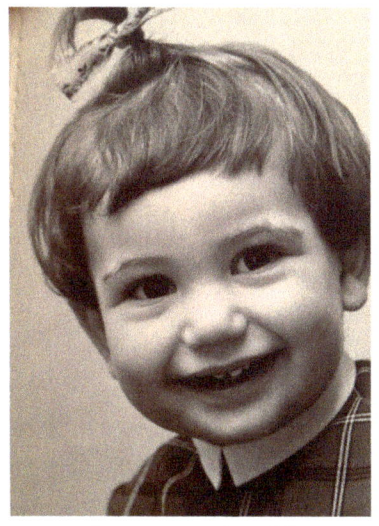

At 18 months old

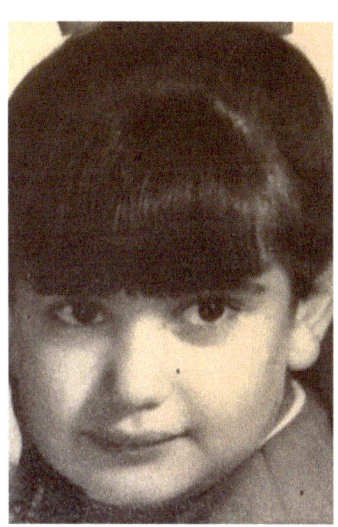

At 4 years old

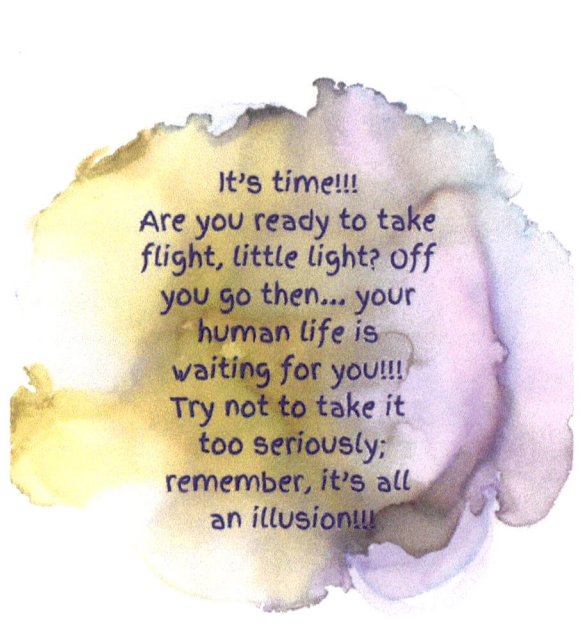

It's time!!!
Are you ready to take flight, little light? Off you go then... your human life is waiting for you!!!! Try not to take it too seriously; remember, it's all an illusion!!!

1
The Beginning

My Protectors

Welcome to the world! On December 19th, 1963, I was born. A long awaited first child and first grandchild. As a toddler I don't have to many memories of my life, but the one that sticks out the most, is needing to feel safe.

From as young as two years old, I can remember seeing people sitting at the end of my bed or next to me when I played. They looked older than my grandparents and so I saw them as the older ones. They would often just sit with me and pass me toys. My favorite playtime was to have high tea with my two friends–Teddy Rosebud and Jackie, my Barbie doll, that I loved to dress up. I would lay out a beautiful tablecloth on the carpet of my bedroom, and on it would be plates of playdough cakes, sandwiches, and cups of lemonade. Of course, I invited the older ones too. I felt so much love coming from them even at that young age I knew they were my protectors.

To me, my world felt normal. It wasn't until I was around 5 years old that I realized no one else could see what

The Paintbrush

I was seeing. I later found out the older ones who played with me were no longer alive; they were my deceased great-grandparents. Once I understood this, my inner world slowly became more and more private, more and more isolated.

World of Imagination

I stayed connected to my intuition which showed up when I played dress-up. I would imagine that I lived in a beautiful palace with my mum and dad, the King and Queen. In my imagination, I was the princess. I would change my outfits for all the parties I attended at least four or five times a day.

My poor mum would often say, "Where is she now? She is so quiet. Please tell me she isn't changing again!" And, of course, I was.

Today I am sure if I asked that little girl why she loved to play so much, she would probably say, *who wouldn't want to play and create a wonderful imaginary world where you can have high tea with angels, fairies, teddies, and Barbie dolls?* As kids, we get it. We are in the moment, and we don't need to analyze why we love what we love. We just know that we do. But then we gradually forget; we stop connecting to our inner world and stop hearing the confident voice that proclaims, *just because I love it!*

What happens to detach us from the experiences of fun, carefree play, and connecting to our imagination? What happens to make us forget the power and wisdom within us? Is it the programming of others telling us how we are supposed to be, who we are supposed to be, and how we are supposed to behave? Maybe it's all the above and more.

1 | The Beginning

For the first four years of my life, I was the only child and the only grandchild. My parents are second-generation English; my true heritage and roots come from different parts of Europe. My father, a highly educated, brilliant man, was a chartered accountant. I remember as early as three years old, my dad would come home every night from work, put me to bed, and tell me one of his made-up bedtime stories that would start with "Can you imagine…." It would always be about the monkey on the train and the mischief he got into. He planted the storyteller seed in me.

My mum was a stay-at-home wife. As a child, one of my favorite memories was making chocolate cake together and then my mum allowing me to lick all the yummy batter off the spoon, raw eggs and all! It's funny the memories that stick out so vividly in our minds!

My paternal Grandfather, Harry, passed away when I was three. My father's mother, my Nanny Milly, and my mother's parents—Papa Ralph and Nana Lilly—were a huge part of my childhood. Every week on a Friday night, we would go to my Nana Lily and Papa Ralph's home together with my Nanny Milly for Shabbat dinner.

After eating, I would always disappear. "Where is she now?" I can hear my mum asking! I was always in my favorite place—in front of my Nana Lily's Art Deco mirror in my grandparents' bedroom, playing with my Nana's jewelry. I loved to try on her mink stoles, her high heels, her long silk gloves, and wear her bright red lipstick from ear to ear! I would daydream and imagine I was as beautiful as my Nana Lily. I felt so special. It's an incredible blessing to have these memories.

The Paintbrush

My Papa Ralph was my hero! He taught me how to play gin rummy cards. Of course, my winnings were always a bag of my favorite candy—pear drops.

Every time I visited them around 4 pm, we would play a game of cards. The table would be set up with a special tablecloth, which was very stylish, and they would both have an aperitif, normally a glass of sherry, accompanied by a bowl of olives and nuts. My Papa Ralph's pride and joy was his antique drinking cellarette which was already 50 years old back then. Every time he opened it, all I could smell was the sweet blends of alcohol he had inside it. I had my very own decanter that had my virgin sherry in it. With great flourish, my Papa would pour me a drink of my virgin sherry and, using a silver toothpick, elegantly put a morello cherry on the top of my little cut glass. I felt so special, loved, and grown-up. My grandparents were the best, and those fabulous memories will live in my heart forever.

Safe to Ask Why

In my world of imagination, everything was possible. *No* was not in my vocabulary. Like most children, being told *no* wasn't what I wanted to hear.

When a sensitive child is told no, and the tone in which it is said has frustration, a child feels dismissed and unheard.

When I was told no, I would want to understand *why is it a no?* And always the answer would be the same, "Because I said so. Don't ask me again."

If I did ask again, I would hear the angry, frustrated tone, "Be quiet now! I said *no!* How many times do I need to say it? *No* is the answer!" My mum called me stubborn and strong-willed.

1 | The Beginning

For most adults, life can be busy, stressful, and sometimes full of anxiety. It is far easier and quicker to say *no* than take the time to explain why. As intuitive souls, children sense the stress and anxiety within others that they then internalize and absorb as their own. They think *it must be my fault that they are upset, I must have done something wrong.* This creates a ripple effect of stress and anxiety within the child's mind that becomes the springboard into their adult mind.

Repeatedly saying no and not answering the why and getting angry transfers to the child a feeling that they are being naughty.

But are they being naughty? Maybe they are just asking a question so they can understand.

Learning to feel safe to ask questions instills in the child a belief in themselves and gives them the confidence to speak up. It's a huge part of validation! This is the support and teaching that they need.

Adults often underestimate the intelligence of a child. Parents are the child's first teacher and saying *no* without an explanation is not enough. Patiently and lovingly taking the time to explain is the key to nourishing a child's healthy emotional mindset.

Everything we do and say is an energy exchange. How we exchange energy with a child is how they begin to internalize the belief about themselves as they grow up.

A frustrated energy exchange starts as a small weed in the garden of a child's mind that, if it is not understood, will eventually create a belief pattern of self-doubt that then affects self-worth. This then depletes a child's awareness of the power they have within themselves and disconnects them from their true source. This is where destructive behaviors often begin.

The Paintbrush

No! has no validation. Asking the question *why* has.

Today's parents understand this better. They take time to be present and give their children suggestions of alternative possibilities rather than just saying *no*. By parenting this way, they are helping the growth of healthy, curious minds.

Being present with your children and giving them the power to feel safe enough to ask any question is the best seed you can plant in their garden of possibilities. They will reap a future full of success, wisdom, compassion, self-belief, and self-worth.

Forming Belief Patterns

It's so interesting to see from a young age how our belief patterns are formed. First comes the programming that we are taught by others, mainly about what to believe and what to see as right and wrong. We are taught to strive to be the best, to do our best, and to be seen as perfect. Judging ourselves and believing other people's interpretations of us are true. What happens when your heart doesn't feel something you are doing is right? What then? Do you still do it? To please others? To be seen as perfect? To not be judged? Oh, that word, *judged*!

Our human life, our complete human existence, is based on stories that are handed down to us from generation to generation! These stories become our beliefs, our truths, and our values.

At around seven years old, we enter a sleep state, forgetting that before this age we know exactly who we are on a deeper level of awareness. In our sleep state, we forget that we are masterful creators. We forget the power we hold. We close ourselves off from our infinite existence, our omnipresence of pure light. We lose touch with our supreme knowledge and

1 | The Beginning

the wisdom that lies within us. We buy into just being human and learn to play small.

We are far bigger and more powerful than we realize.

Through my own evolution, what became clearer to me as I started to spiritually grow was that I never lost touch with my inner knowledge, my inner voice, and my intuition. I never closed them down. I just got caught up in misconceptions, and untrue beliefs I had about myself. Only when I started to weed my emotional garden did I become aware of my true self on an even deeper level.

The Paintbrush

Reflection of Wisdom

*Life is a blooming flower
in the garden of our minds.
First a seed is planted.
Over time it grows.
Weathering the storms of change.
Through rain, snow, and drought
Until one day, the sun appears again.*

*I dreamt of a day when I saw myself
through the eyes of my divine self.
The day my heart skipped a beat and
danced in the beauty of acceptance and love.
The day when I could throw
all those old beliefs away
and bathe in the joy of me.*

1 | The Beginning

This painting is called *The Creation of Life*. It's reflects the awareness that life is forever moving forward step by step.

2
The Wheels of Life Roll

By the time I was four years old, my brother Richard was born, and I instinctively became his big sister protector.

One day my mother overheard me talking. She thought I was pretending to speak to somebody until she heard a voice speaking to me from the other end of the phone. Shocked, my mother asked the person, "Who are you?"

"I am the headmistress of a school," she replied, "and I have been having a delightful conversation with your daughter about enrolling her brother into my school and how she shares her birthday with her daddy! How old is your daughter?" she asked.

I was only five years old at the time. The headmistress went on to tell my mother that I was an exceptionally bright child and that maybe one day I would attend her school.

It's incredible to think back to that experience; how did I even find the phone number to call the headmistress? And how important it must have been for me to tell her about my dad?

Being born on my dad's birthday is very special to me. What's even more special is our birth numbers are the same.

The Paintbrush

My dad was born on December 19, 1936, and I was born on December 19, 1963.

My dad was a perfect student and won many awards in school. He even won an award for his handwriting. On the other hand, I struggled with reading and writing. My dad's brain is about logic, and mine is about creativity. His value system was all about academics. As a child I never felt I could come close to meeting the expectations I believed he had of me.

Dyslexia in 1968

At 5 years of age, I was enrolled in a strict private prep school close to my home, where most of the children in our neighborhood attended. I went there until I was 10 years old. Attending that school gave me a lot of emotional and mental anxiety. There were consequences if the students did not behave well and pay attention. The girls were punished with the slipper and the boys with the cane. Being disciplined like this terrified me.

I have dyslexia. In 1968, dyslexia was not common knowledge, so it went undiagnosed until well into my adulthood. Everyone assumed that I was plain lazy. Dyslexia affects people in different ways. It involves difficulty reading, decoding speech sounds, and understanding how they relate to letters and words.

I would get words and numbers mixed up, making reading almost impossible. My brain just couldn't absorb what I was hearing. This also made learning how to spell very difficult for me.

2 | The Wheels of Life Roll

Mr. Peebles was the headmaster of my prep school and was known for being very strict. The thought of being called into his office and seeing the slipper sent shivers of fear down my 5-year-old spine.

One day, Ms. Margaret, my year-one teacher, was at the chalkboard teaching about capital letters. Chalk was everywhere as she wrote sentence after sentence on the board, explaining the rules of capitalization. One by one we were all called up to write a sentence. When it was my turn, I remember writing the first letter of each word of the sentence in capitals.

This is simply how my brain had interpreted it. "You're not paying attention! If you're not going to listen to what I am teaching you, you can leave the room!" said Ms. Margaret. She made me stand outside the door until the class was over.

I felt utterly embarrassed that the whole classroom saw this. Standing outside the door for the remainder of the lesson, I felt confused, sad, and scared. I wanted so badly to be clever. The thought of disappointing my parents and wanting to please my teacher would consume me. I would think, *how can I try harder and get it right today? I need my brain to pay attention.*

This affected me so much that I would frequently become sick. Tonsillitis from three years old was a big part of my childhood until I had them removed at 18.

Other times when I wasn't sick, the anxiety about going to school would be so intense that I would put my head on the radiator until it was burning hot. I would then go and find my mum. When the thermometer read 100 degrees, my mum would say, "Oh, you're not well enough to go to school today, darling. You must have a bug; you better stay home

The Paintbrush

with me." By the middle of the morning, my temperature would miraculously disappear, and I would be well enough to go grocery shopping with her. And, of course, we would always finish up at the bakery shop, where she would buy me my favorite butter cookie.

I dreaded getting my end-of-year report cards. They would always say, "Poor attendance due to missing too much school." "Needs to try harder." "Doesn't listen in class." "Doesn't pay attention." Hearing my parents read this to me would make me sad and feel even more stupid. In the late 60s, altering the teaching method so I could understand what I was being taught was not an option.

While no two brains are alike, the brains of people with dyslexia are distinctly different. It has been scientifically proven that dyslexic brains work five times harder than an average brain. Because of this, my brain, to this day, still works much faster than most average people. However, I didn't know how to process information then, so I felt overwhelmed. When a child gets overwhelmed with learning challenges, they shut down, and anxiety takes over. This was the beginning of me withdrawing into myself and creating my own coping mechanisms.

Today I am so grateful that the schooling system in England and worldwide has come a long way. There is much more awareness, care, and attention to children's well-being and to the signs of learning differences, anxiety, and mental health issues.

2 | The Wheels of Life Roll

Convent, Hebrew School & Shopping

By the time I was ten, my sister Charlotte was born—my own real-life doll. With ten years between us, as my baby sister grew up, she saw me as her protector. I was her big sis, and to this day, I still am!

It was also around this time at 10 years old that my prep school was facing closure. In England, you must take a written entrance exam to attend secondary school at 11 years old. As I was only ten years old, my parents had to find a school that would accommodate a child like me as they knew I would never be able to pass a written exam.

Thank God for my mother. She saw the movie *"The Nun's Story"* when it came out in 1959. The star was Audrey Hepburn playing the role of a caring, patient, and kind nun. Her memory of that movie provided the insight she needed—she knew exactly where to send me to school. But she was also clear about the fact that she wasn't sending her Jewish daughter to become a nun at the local private convent.

So, my weekdays were spent in the convent, and I attended Hebrew school on Sundays. Saturdays were reserved for my other religion: shopping. My dad loved to joke about this: "Best bury me at the mall. At least then, I can guarantee you'll remember to visit me."

And so, I went to the nunnery run by order of the Dominican nuns and Franciscan friars. A seed was planted that would later grow and blossom into a catalyst for change at a significant time in my life.

The Paintbrush

At the convent, Jewish girls were not expected to attend mass. Yet sometimes, I felt drawn to the chapel and would go there just to sit and feel the energy of peace. I didn't see the Catholic religion one way and the Jewish religion a different way. It wasn't a question of I'm this, and you are that. My heart knew then that many roads lead to God, and I wanted to understand them all.

What I have come to understand is this: everything is a divine plan, a precise journey, that when the time is right, what we have planted will blossom and grow. The rhythm of life is perfect; it's a cycle of events. Nothing can be rushed; it's not in our time! We think it is, but honestly, it is not. It's in God's time! Think—Trust—Allow—Receive!

And so, at ten years old, one of these profound divine plans was planted as a seed within me that would take another 30 years to come to fruition.

While sitting in the chapel one day, I saw this beautiful light shining through the stained-glass windows. As I closed my eyes, I felt warm rays of light shining on me, and I heard a voice that sounded as if it was coming from within me say, *don't be sad, child; we know it's hard. We understand your loneliness and struggles, but keep going; even though its hard, don't give up. You will understand more by the time you are 40 years old; this we promise.* And while I felt this was strange, as I was only ten and 40 was a long way away, hearing this message somehow brought me great comfort. It was also around this time that I starting to develop a deeper connection to my intuition and my inner voice.

The Sound of My Inner Voice

Let's pause a moment because I feel it's important to explain what my inner voice sounds like. It's beyond just hearing the words spoken; it's far more profound. It's a feeling that something more significant than my human mind is communicating with me. When I hear a message, I know it comes from a deeper level within me. It sounds like a soft whisper, guiding me to pay attention, reminding me to take a breath, to become quiet in my mind, and listen. As a sensitive soul, the gift of this knowing and presence gave me comfort and guidance, especially when I would take things personally and to heart.

You're Too Soft, Toughen Up!

Witnessing my reaction to people's behavior and events, my mum would often tell me that I was too soft and that I needed to get thicker skin. "The world out there is cruel; you need to toughen up," she would say. Today, I know that not having the ability to toughen up was my saving grace. I have come to understand that my intuition and inner voice would never have connected with me on the level that it still does, to this day, if I had become tougher. My intuition helped me navigate my inner world at that time as a sensitive, empathic soul.

Staying vulnerable was part of my growth and experience and helped me learn compassion, self-love, and inner wisdom.

The Paintbrush

And although, for a long time, being sensitive did play havoc with my belief system, thank God it was not embedded deep enough to make an ever-lasting effect on me.

First, you learn to crawl, then you know to walk, then you learn to run, but when do you learn to fly? At school, by now, I was a master of flying. The only difference was I wasn't standing outside the door anymore. Instead, I was in the back of the classroom in my imagination. I imagine flying out of the classroom window, returning just in time for the lessons to be over.

Around 11 years of age, I finally started learning to read and write properly. As for spelling, forget it! My spelling ability arrived only a few years ago, and even today, as I write this book, I love typing words, only to discover that autocorrect doesn't believe they exist! Maybe they do, just not on this planet.

Blessed by the Pope

As I entered my teenage years, two significant life experiences happened to me at 13. One was when I met Pope John Paul II in 1979.

The school organized a field trip to Rome to visit the Pope, and then from there, we would visit Florence. Little did I know another seed was about to be planted. I vividly remember that audience with the Pope—100 girls, the nuns, and me—the only Jewish girl. What an experience! The room was very private, just for us alone. Many of my friends back home were Catholic, so I bought them rosary beads at the Vatican and held them in my hands as His Holiness put his hand on my head, said a blessing over me, and crossed himself.

2 | The Wheels of Life Roll

I saw this as a beautiful gesture of love for me to receive the Pope's blessing and for my friends to obtain it, too. This was the highlight of my experience in Rome.

Saved by Angels

The second significant event was my first near-death experience when I was run over by a car. I genuinely believe that an angel or a team of angels saved my life that day.

I was walking home alone late in the afternoon after spending some time with a friend during our summer holiday. Three construction workers were wolf-whistling at me as they walked right behind me. This triggered a feeling of sheer panic from a terrifying incident that had happened the night before.

My friends and I were hanging out at our Jewish social club when a gang of boys with batons and glass bottles raided the building. My friends and I were scared and ran for our lives. I had not had time to recover from this trauma. The construction workers intimidated me so much that I panicked and walked straight into the middle of the narrow road and just stood there frozen. A bus was coming towards me in the opposite direction, so I took a step back, and as I did, a car hit me. I was thrown over the whole length of the car and spun in the air before hitting the ground.

The driver kept going. How does someone leave a person lying on the road? But they did. The men who were wolf-whistling kept walking. They never came to my rescue. An elderly couple who lived on that road heard the accident and came running out to see what happened. They called the police and my parents.

The Paintbrush

With no witnesses, the police had no case, and the driver was never found. What I know for sure is that my life was saved by angels that day. I sustained some severe injuries, but believe me, not many survive that type of accident. It was indeed a miracle that I did.

My left leg was the most damaged from the impact of me hitting the ground so hard. I was left with a nine-inch distended lump on the side of my leg. The orthopedic specialist taking care of me told my mother the only way to mend this was to cut it out, which would leave me with a nine-inch scar. For my mother, that scar was not an option, and she went on a mission to find a better solution. She found a fantastic plastic surgeon that performed a new and untested procedure called liposuction, one he had never performed before.

In the Royal Orthopedic hospital, I was the guinea pig for this operation that took him three hours to perform. My recuperation time was two weeks lying flat in a bed with my leg attached to a drain.

Today, I thank God for both my mum and the angel surgeon. I have no scar on my leg except for a tiny mark where he performed the procedure. This in itself is another amazing miracle.

Report Card Mishaps

My end-of-year school report cards were still a cause of worry for me. The thought of giving them to my parents, especially my dad, would cause me a lot of sleepless nights.

Many mishaps befell those cards, and most of the time, they would never quite make it into my parents' hands.

One time I remember going home and telling my mum how, by accident, I had spilled hot coffee all over my math report card, which was totally unreadable.

Another time I lost my backpack with all my report cards in it. I had accidentally thrown it over a fence, where it landed in a ditch, and because a bull was in the field, I couldn't get to it. I got into a lot of trouble for this one!

Even an alien abduction happened once, where I saw my English report card beamed up!

Bless my poor parents, they would call the school to have the report cards sent directly to the house, but even they, in the end, gave up! They knew that what I didn't have in grades, I certainly made up for in personality.

Empath & Illusions

To my friends and family, no one saw me as unhappy. Why would I show them what I was feeling? With the mask of illusion firmly on my face, I was full of bubbling fun and joy, the leader of the pack, the best friend, sister, daughter, the one person who never let you down. Yet, inside of me, I carried this deep sadness—a yearning to be in a world that vibrated at the same level of frequency as me. I just wanted to belong, but belong to what?

I learned that feeling and pretending to be happy takes a lot of courage and energy. If you believe you are weak because you are forcing yourself to be happy, you are not; it is a sign of strength, determination, and focus on your part, that you want something more than what you feel. This is your inner will pushing through you. When you become more aware of

The Paintbrush

this, you awaken a deeper connection to your internal wisdom, your inner voice, and your own inner universe.

I have come to understand that I am an empath. When someone is sad, I can *feel* it. So often, I would feel confused or angry and believe it was my issues or my stuff that caused it! I wish I'd known then that I was absorbing other people's pain and that it wasn't mine to hold onto.

Are you an empath? If yes, right now, put your hand on your heart and feel the power that surrounds you at this moment. This power is your auric field protecting you. There is an exercise I do, to keep my energy field safe. Before I step out of the house each day, I step into my astronaut outfit and zip myself up into it, all the way above my head. This protects my auric field from any outside influences. This helps shield me from energies that do not support a sensitive soul. For an empath, this is very important.

Learning to stay strong and clear of energy vampires is the key to maintaining your power. Only when you are clear and not drained from other people's energy can you know yourself.

Getting to know our true authentic self is a journey of self-discovery that starts the day we are born. Although most of the time, we are totally unaware of this. The game of life is our greatest teacher.

We believe many different parts of ourselves make up who we are. First is the *identity part* that holds the belief of who and what we are. Second is the *judgment part* where we buy into lies about ourselves that are not true. The third is the *wishing part*, which is the part that believes that if only we were different, we would be accepted and loved. On the one hand, I knew I was connected to something deeper within myself, yet at times I yearned for something more–to be accepted just for me.

Self-Bullying

Anorexia and bulimia can go hand-in-hand with learning challenges, low self-esteem, and lack of self-worth. As a little girl, I was super skinny, but as I matured and went through puberty, I started to gain weight. I wasn't comfortable with the changes in my body. I wished I could get into the skinny girls' clothes I saw on TV and in magazines. Body image is a mental picture we create of ourselves, which, sadly, most of the time is not true. In the society that we live in today, being skinny is seen as perfect and beautiful. This is an unrealistic expectation that we put on ourselves. This mindset can eventually lead to distress and self-loathing, which, if not addressed, leads to self-bullying.

Believing that someone else's negative, hurtful words are true is very destructive. This is why I created Be Wellness Mind, a platform dedicated to teaching a technique called Intuitive Mind Space™, which expands your beliefs into infinite possibilities and self-love. You can learn more about this on my website *TiaCrystal.com.*

I have learned some tough, painful lessons throughout my life, but what I have come to understand is this: nothing is ever quite what it seems—not our beliefs, our judgments, other people's judgments, hurtful comments, and definitely not the untrue ideas we have about ourselves. These misconceptions are old, out-of-date painful memories buried deep within us. If they are not healed, they will create havoc in all aspects of

The Paintbrush

our relationships with ourselves and others. First, you must love yourself, only then can you love another.

A memory deep within me that I had to heal was that in addition to feeling stupid, I also felt fat and ugly. I remember the pain of buying clothes with my mum and having them not fit me. My friends were wearing the most fabulous outfits, and I wanted to wear them, too.

I remember one afternoon, my mum and I went to a trendy boutique to buy me something nice to wear to our local Jewish club that I would go to with my friends every Saturday night. I chose a few pretty tops and a fabulous pair of size 14 designer jeans to try on. I envisioned myself wearing them, thinking how lovely and accepted I would feel. In the fitting room I tried on the clothes and one by one handed them back to my mum as none of them fit. I went home so broken hearted that I hid in my room and ate for comfort.

Today, I understand that the extra weight around me was a layer of protection caused by my thoughts and beliefs about myself. Food was my comfort when I was sad. Food brought me joy; it filled me up. It was a quick fix that only lasted a little while, but the weight lasted a long time.

The society I grew up in focused on looking and dressing perfect and being the ideal weight. The social pressure I lived under was constant and intense. So, I just needed to be skinny. In my mind, I believed that if I was, I would be loved.

I had heard from one of my friends about diet pills, so I pleaded with my mum to take me to the doctor, and she did. I started taking the pills, but my sensitive body reacted to them, so I had to stop. It wasn't until I was in the process of my own healing that I learned my emotional self was undernourished.

2 | The Wheels of Life Roll

Nothing would work until this part of me was addressed and healed.

In my head I kept hearing, *run, rabbit, run rabbit, run, run, run!* I was running from myself, of course!

I started dieting at age 16, and with the weight loss came the fear of gaining it back. And so began my eating disorders—anorexia and bulimia—that would last throughout my teens and into my late 20s.

Weight Watchers taught me how to count calories, and salad had almost none. It gave the appearance that I was eating a lot, but I was actually starving myself. Having bulimia and anorexia was a big shame for me and one I tried to keep very well hidden. After our family meals, my parents would comment on how quickly I would have to excuse myself and go to the bathroom. I was very conscious of this dark secret as it was my own private cross to bear and one I worked hard on keeping to myself.

I needed to feel in control, and food was my way of feeling that. This gave me the illusion of being empowered, but slowly even that would slip away, and I would eat uncontrollably. When I went on a binge, my brain would scream at me, *that will make you fat, stop!* But by then, I was in such a deep fog focused only on feeding the emptiness within me that I didn't want to hear it. The feeling of fullness would only last a few minutes, then with a vengeance, the sense of guilt would take over, and I would be angry at myself for eating.

Chocolate was my emotional comfort. I remember eating three pieces and saying to myself, *that's it, you got your fix, no more.* But before I knew it, this uncontrollable feeling of needing to eat more was so intense that I would devour the

The Paintbrush

whole bag of chocolate. Once I felt that emotional connection to happiness, I would stop. Then I would feel guilty. So, I would purge it. Then I would feel safe again, and then I would feel confused and ashamed for having eaten at all.

Starvation - binge - purge - this was the cycle I was caught up in for many, many years.

My emotional needs were starved of acceptance, while my outer world felt totally out of control. I believed I wasn't good enough and was reminded of this daily at school. In one breath, I would be told by my teachers what I wasn't doing right, and then in another, I would hear my soft-spoken voice of my inner voice, telling me, *it's all going to be ok!*

The Cherokee refer to this as the two wolves in our mind. So, which wolf within my mind was I feeding the most?

Yet, all of this didn't stop me from falling head over heels in love and having my first real boyfriend.

Picture this: I am at a costume party for a friend's 16th birthday, all dressed in a clown outfit—big red nose, shiny dungarees, rosy cheeks, and a giant curly wig. Hiding in a clown suit, little, stupid, no qualifications me meets Mr. Popular, Mr. Brilliant, Mr. Oxford, Here-I-Come, Mr. Handsome. And he falls madly in love with me! Me! I couldn't believe it. We had a romance full of innocent puppy love and living in the moment. I felt beautiful, adored, and validated. I was so giddy in love that anorexia and bulimia were not my focus. I was eating normally and not gaining weight. My heart was happy.

And then, ten months later, just like that, it was over. Abrupt, painful, and heartbreaking.

Reflection of Wisdom

I cry a tear for me,
I cry a tear for you
but most of all
I cry a tear alone,
please, someone
show me where I belong.

3
Please, Someone, Show Me the Way!

Goodbye School

The year is 1978. I am 15 and supposed to be studying for my final year 12 exams along with all my other fellow classmates.

Instead, I decided it was time to leave my education behind me. I knew I would never pass my exams, so why try to just fail? No way, I had the tee-shirt for that one. It was time to leave school, go into the world, and find a job. I discussed this with my parents, and they agreed. All they wanted was for me to be happy.

I kept hearing, *run rabbit, run rabbit, run, run, run!*

But run where? My self-talk was full of questions: *What do I do now? Where do I belong? Please, someone, show me the way.*

The Paintbrush

#1 Hairstylist

I decided to become a hairdresser as I was good at styling my friend's hair. I was an apprentice hairdresser at a salon near my home for a year. Then, at 16, I applied to a salon in Knightsbridge and got the job.

It was one of the top hair salons in London. The owner Mario was a judge at all the international hair shows and would style the hair of the rich and famous aristocracy. The salon was one of the first in London to have a spa, and high society English ladies would spend the entire day there. We were one of the pioneer leaders in facials and body treatments for cellulite.

I still had two years of studying to become a hairdresser. But within a year, I became the assistant to Mario. He saw the talent within me, how my eye looked at a client and could see the finished results. He said I was a born natural hairdresser and trusted me, so he would cut and color his clients and then pass them over to me to finish the blow-dry. My creativity came out in this as well as in pin curls and perms and big bouffant hair with lots of backcombing.

By the time I was 18, I was a stylist myself. Even though I had to take two trains and spend 3 hours a day traveling to the salon, I loved it! Being creative nourished my emotional soul.

Until one tragic day, July 20, 1982. As the Queen's soldiers left Knightsbridge Barracks for the changing of the guard ceremony in Whitehall, a bomb was detonated that killed four soldiers and seven horses. Two hours later, another bomb was fired at the bandstand in Regents Park, killing seven innocent band members and injuring 30 more.

3 | Please, Someone, Show Me the Way!

My salon was only a few miles away. One minute I was blow drying my client's hair, and the next minute I felt the ground shake beneath me and suddenly saw the front windows explode and shattered glass everywhere. And then, silence as if I was watching a movie in slow-motion before pandemonium screaming and wailing sirens took over. I didn't have a cell phone back then, and the landlines were down, so I spent five long hours in a panic trying to reach my parents to tell them I was unharmed.

The Knightsbridge tragedy made me reevaluate my priorities. So, I decided to shift gears, even though I loved hairdressing, and go in a new direction.

Again, I heard, *run, rabbit, run rabbit, run, run, run!* Where was I to go next?

To… The Nut House.

The Nut House

A mental asylum? No, this nut house sold nuts. I was told about a sales assistant job at a beautiful, elegant retail store that sold over 50 varieties of nuts from all around the world. This was a huge novelty in London at that time. And so off I went for an interview and was immediately offered the job.

Remember, only after events have unfolded do you truly understand the journey. I loved working at this lovely shop and believed my role was only to serve the customers; I left the design of those nutty gifts to those better suited to the role. I was confident about being a hairdresser, but now I was faced with a new challenge. My old programming was coming up again. *What did I know about gift baskets?*

The Paintbrush

One day my boss told me, "You want to work here? You need to learn every part of this company. You need to know how to make the baskets, tie the ribbon, make the lavish bows, and all within 5 minutes."

So, I pushed myself and rose to the challenge. I would practice making the bows at home at night until I perfected them. I learned how to create elegant bows out of a mass of 100 strands of thin pieces of ribbon. I tapped into my hairdressing eye for design and would style and cut a bow as if I was styling hair. They were so gorgeous that customers would keep them to reuse. Within 6 months of working there, my boss was so impressed with my work ethic that he made me the manager of the shop.

Three years later the company was up for sale, and so my parents and close friends invested in me, and I became the owner of The Nut Shop. I worked even harder at growing the business. Now the responsibility for success was entirely on my shoulders. The company was thriving, but underneath, I felt at times so overwhelmed. How I appeared to the outside world— a young entrepreneur with a successful business— was not how I saw myself. Those voices of criticism and self-doubt sometimes would rear their ugly heads, especially when I was tired from working 18 hours daily. They would wreak havoc in my mind saying, *how can you possibly be successful? How do you deserve to own your company at 22 years old?*

3 | Please, Someone, Show Me the Way!

Power of the Ego

Never underestimate the power of the ego. When you give it the talking stick, it never stops. My ego knew where to poke me—straight in my fragile self-worth and flimsy self-esteem, robbing me of my true, unique, magnificent self.

When you are blinded to the beauty of who you are, your choices can be painful. They are not based on self-worth but on what you believe you are not worthy of!

Within 5 years of leaving school, I couldn't understand how I could have so much success. It was time to learn the life lesson of worthiness and self-love.

You tend to attract unhealthy, narcissistic relationships when you believe you do not deserve better. This happened to me, and it was one of the hardest life lessons for me to learn. In this next chapter, I share how it nearly cost me my life.

The Paintbrush

Reflection of Wisdom

*Through many doors I will go
until I find my true home.*

3 | Please, Someone, Show Me the Way!

Allegresse represents the gift of awareness. All is in grace. This heart is overflowing with the abundance of grace. We are alive, vibrant, and full of joy.

4
Motherhood and the Will to Live

My First Marriage

Naiveté is the purest part of one's heart. I have been brought up to believe that marriage is a sacred commitment. A husband loves his wife, is loyal, caring, supportive, your best friend, and the one person who would protect you above all else. It's a partnership where two people come together to honor and cherish each other, just like my parents do to this day, after 60 years of marriage.

What I envisioned and what really happened in my first marriage were two different things. The signs were there initially; I just refused to see them or even believe them. I thought that if I could love my husband enough, I could change him. As an empathic soul, I was a prime candidate for a narcissistic relationship. Because of this, I chose to ignore my intuition and gut feelings.

The Paintbrush

He was handsome, elegant, and sophisticated, and I was drawn in by his charm and the attention he paid me. My struggles with dyslexia, bulimia and anorexia left me yearning to be loved and adored. He would tell me how beautiful I was, filling a big hole in me. Whenever we were out, he would tell people, "Aren't I the lucky one to have someone like her?" It wasn't until much later in our relationship that I realized it was all about making himself look better.

By the age of 23, most of my friends were getting married. That's how it was back then. I would daydream about that, too. What dress I would wear and how I would be a loving wife, making my husband happy and a beautiful home full of children. I envisioned a marriage like my parents had. I had been dreaming about this since I was a little girl. So, when he asked me to marry him, I said, "Yes!"

My parents asked me if I was sure. My inner voice was screaming at me, *no, don't marry him!* I chose to ignore them both.

Trauma Begins

During our first few years of marriage, he went from job to job. They wouldn't last. He would tell me things like, "It's not my fault that they don't appreciate me." "They don't see my talent." "I'm better than this." I didn't know it then, but all the while, he was borrowing money from our friends.

Once I overheard a heated conversation on the phone about money. The person on the other line said, "If you don't pay, I'm coming after you!" I didn't know what it was about and didn't ask him either.

4 | Motherhood and the Will to Live

People would come knocking at our door. He would tell me it was a client and that he needed to talk to them privately. Then, he would invite them into the living room and offer them a glass of wine. I later found out these were Bailiffs, and he was schmoozing with them, telling them a story that wasn't true, to buy himself more time.

He was in charge of the mail. I was never allowed to go to the mailbox. I did this by mistake once, and he said, "How dare you not obey what I tell you to do. You are not allowed to go to the mailbox; only I am." If at any time, I didn't listen to what he told me to do, he would get furious.

His Porsche was his pride and joy, and he would spend hours every Saturday polishing it. I was never allowed to drive it or make any mess in it. It felt like he was more in love with the thought of his status, his looks, and what he had than with me!

On the rare occasion that I let him know I was unhappy, that I couldn't take it anymore and that I was going to leave him, he would get so distraught that he would sit on the windowsill of our three-story home, threatening to jump out of the window.

I would sit there frozen in fear.

He would tell me, "This will be your fault, and you'll be the one to blame." I would be shaking, crying, and pleading for him to stop. Other times I would hide in the cupboard so he couldn't find me. Even though I knew it was never going to change, I wanted to believe maybe it would. He was lovely when he was nice, but that wasn't often and didn't last long.

I thought that if we could just have a baby, then everything would be perfect. I wanted to believe this; after all, he was my husband. The only thing controlling my anorexia and bulimia at that time was my yearning to have a baby.

The Paintbrush

Only after I started doing some intense inner healing work did I learn that narcissistic people lead others to believe they are going mad. An empath tends to want to heal the world, and they tend to choose relationships with people who need healing. I've come to understand that narcissistic people feed off of sensitive souls with big, kind forgiving hearts. These soft-hearted people believe all they need to do is love that person enough to make it all better.

Although I was successful in my business, I didn't dare tell my parents I was in an unhappy marriage. I never wanted them to worry. I wanted them to believe that everything was ok. My husband's egotistical behavior was indeed my greatest teacher, as it would one day put me on the path to learning how to love myself.

Life or Death

It took a few years to become pregnant. When I finally did, I was over the moon with happiness! I hoped being pregnant would make our relationship better. Sadly, I was wrong.

One Sunday afternoon, we were over at our close friends for tea, and I was not feeling well. I was lying on the sofa having strange stabbing pains in my stomach, which I thought maybe was due to constipation. I ate some prunes, but that didn't help. After a while, our friends told my husband that I looked very pale and that we should probably call my gynecologist as the pain wasn't going away. He replied, "I am sure it is nothing." However, our friends didn't feel that and insisted he call. Finally, he did. My gynecologist told him to bring me to the hospital immediately.

4 | Motherhood and the Will to Live

My husband drove me to the hospital like a lunatic, with the hazard lights flashing, running red lights, and beeping his horn at intersections.

I arrived at the hospital at 11 pm. My gynecologist had an ultrasound set up and waiting. The scan showed that I had a mass attached to my womb; that was all the radiologist could tell me.

I was only 26 weeks into my pregnancy. My gynecologist asked my husband if I had been under any extreme stress. He replied, "Yes, she has been working hard at her shop and getting the baby stuff ready." He told my husband to call my parents immediately, as I needed to undergo a life-threatening operation. A gangrenous fibroid was attached to my womb, and my white blood cells were seriously elevated.

By 1 am, my parents arrived at the hospital and were told I was to undergo a life-saving operation. Before the surgery, my mother told me, "You are going to fight to stay alive. I am not going to lose you, and you are not going to lose your baby."

We had a choice, my baby and I, in my second near-death experience. We could choose to not return or live to share our life experiences together.

A surgery like mine had never been performed before on a pregnant woman. My baby still in its amniotic sack would have to be removed from my womb so the gangrenous growth could be removed, and then be put back inside!

During my operation, I met my baby in a space full of light. I remember this as if it was yesterday. Neither of us was in physical form; we were both light energy. It was a sacred exchange that we had with each other. I remember sensing turmoil, strength, and deep, deep love. We could see some of

The Paintbrush

our shared life lessons and what we would have to do to face them together.

My baby was given a choice: to come into this world or not.

The operation lasted nine hours. When I came out of it, I was kept in a semi-coma as they wanted to ensure I didn't go into premature labor. This lasted for two weeks. Then, slowly I was allowed to walk a little, and one of the places I loved to visit was the nursery.

One night I couldn't sleep, so I went to watch the nurses feed the newborn babies. I was very excited about becoming a mum and wanted to be the best at it. I sat down on a nursing chair and watched. They were so kind to me. They gave me tips on burping and on how to help a baby if it had colic.

As I got up to leave, I felt something tear in my stomach. I slowly walked back to my room and got in bed, feeling something strange happening around my stitches.

The next day, the pain around my stitches was getting worse. My mother came to visit me, and I told her that something didn't feel right. Unfortunately, she only had half an hour that day to see me, as she had a meeting she needed to go to with my dad.

As she was leaving, she told the nurse to come in and see if everything was ok.

By the time she reached the elevator, she heard code red and turned around to see that it was coming from my room. She ran back to witness blood all over my sheets. Like a zipper, my entire stomach had opened up all the way to my guts. My poor mum stood there in sheer panic as if watching a horror movie while I was screaming from the intense pain and agony.

4 | Motherhood and the Will to Live

Six nurses rushed in, and each held a portion of my stomach together as one of them gave me a sedative shot that knocked me out.

I was rushed to have another six-hour operation to again save our lives. I had a massive infection that was spreading inside my entire body. The doctors started pumping more antibiotics in me and a drug to stop my uterus from going into labor. To stitch me up, the surgeon used the same nylon thread that sailors use on ship's sails. He used plastic tubes around the stitches to keep the stitches strong and intact.

The pain was so intense.

I was finally allowed to leave the hospital and decided it would be easier to go to my parent's house, where my mum, dad, and sister could take care of me. I stayed with them for a month before returning home to prepare the house for my baby.

Where There Is a Will

My parents arranged for an Au Pair to come. I was still weak, and they knew I needed help. She was a lovely young girl from Portugal, she helped me for two hours in the morning and two hours in the evening.

We had so much fun washing all the baby things in preparation for my big day.

Six weeks later, I gave birth to my beautiful, healthy daughter naturally; she weighed a whopping eight pounds, four ounces. When the will is strong, nothing can stop it.

You would have thought that the emotional abuse would have stopped after what I had gone through. But, no, sadly, it did not! During my first few months of motherhood, I developed a lump in my throat that started a thyroid condition.

The Paintbrush

I endured so much trauma but healed from it and learned to become bigger and stronger than the trauma itself. The biggest lesson I learned was that I wasn't to blame. I also knew that forgiveness sets you free, and the person I most needed to forgive was myself.

One day, my husband went to grab our daughter out of my arms because I had done something that annoyed him. That was it, I snapped. That was the final straw. The mother bear in me said, *no more,* and with my daughter in my arms, I walked out the door with my head held high, and I never looked back.

Mother Bear

My precious baby daughter and I went back to live with my parents. It was now my mum, my dad, my Nana Lily (my Papa Ralph had passed away), and my two siblings. My daughter and I shared a bedroom with my amazing sister, who was 17 at the time. And now my baby sister was my baby's babysitter!

I took my daughter with me during the day to The Nut House. To make extra money and care for both of us, I attended a six-month culinary course to become a pastry chef at night. I would make novelty cakes for all my friends' children's birthdays. Creating decorative, happy cakes for children was very healing for me. Again, I was very good at it and loved it. I would take samples of the cakes to The Nut House for my customers to try, and before I knew it, I would have orders of ten cakes and more a month to make.

4 | Motherhood and the Will to Live

Healing the Trauma

The trauma I endured stayed buried for a while, but it soon rose to get my attention. The pain of what I went through made me extra protective of my daughter. Her father was so furious that even though I had left him, he constantly looked at ways to hurt me.

How did I heal? With my loving family by my side and by having good friends who loved me. Through the power of motherhood and the deep desire to ensure that my daughter did not repeat my experiences. Thus, the journey of learning to love myself began. Step-by-step.

One thing I know for sure—when someone tells you to never give up, you must listen to them because you are worthy of happiness. You will go from being a victim of the illusion of beliefs that are not true to becoming victorious and beyond. When transformed, your scars will become the vision of your grace, valor, and inner beauty. This will mold you into a person of substance, someone on a mission to discover your inner power and self-love. This will also guide you to making wiser choices, listening to your inner knowing, and trusting your gut feeling.

So, on that note, do you remember earlier in the book I wrote how events happen in God's time and that only after they unfold can we understand the reasons for some of our life experiences?

Well! Little did I know that the seed of my next marriage had already been planted when I stepped into The Nut House eight years earlier.

The Paintbrush

My Knight in Shining Armor

A neighbor who lived down the street where I lived with my family had an interest in me. And somehow, he had recruited an ally, a spy in my household—my Nana Lily. Picture this: the two of them would arrange a private rendezvous to plan and strategize how a date could happen.

The twist in the plot and a kink in the pipe was that several years before this, I had had a falling out with one of the chocolate distributors who supplied my company for years. Jonathan, the company owner's son, called me one day to tell me they would no longer supply me with chocolate because our account was 30 days overdue. It was business, and sometimes those kinds of things happen. The man who was now chatting up my Nana Lily and trying to get close to me just happened to be that same Jonathan, the son of the man who owned the chocolate company!

I remember saying, "Nana, if you like him that much and think he's such a nice boy, why don't you go on a date with him?" Another friend of mine had already tried to match us, and my response was a firm, "No!" It was all far too embarrassing; I couldn't possibly date him. But he wasn't taking no for an answer, and with my Nana Lily standing by as his spy, we started to date.

A year later, I married Jonathan, who became a wonderful loving father to my daughter, Melissa. The doctors told me it would be unlikely I could ever conceive again because of my first pregnancy complications. Never in my wildest dreams did I believe I would have any more children.

4 | Motherhood and the Will to Live

But at our engagement party, I found out I was pregnant! So, we quickly decided to bring our wedding forward, and six months later, James was born, and we became a family of four. The doctors were obviously wrong because 17 months later, my third child, Joshua, was born, and we became a family of five.

And finally, the rabbit stopped running.

The Paintbrush

Reflection of Wisdom

*And so, her knight in shining armor appeared,
as he bent down to bring her onto his horse
with her precious daughter in her arms,
he said,
"Together we are a family as one."*

4 | Motherhood and the Will to Live

The Birthing Goddess. She represents the new cycles of life and how we as human beings are continually birthing new ideas.

Time to blossom and grow.
Now three little precious
ones to call our own.

5
Growing Into Me

Octopus SuperMum

Life was busy in our household with three children under 5 years of age. I was grateful that I had had seven incredible years being the owner of The Nut Shop, but now my priorities had changed. The Octopus SuperMum hat was firmly placed on my head.

Jonathan and I would joke with each other almost daily that we were living on a fast-moving train, constantly juggling everyone's needs.

Even going to the supermarket with my children was an expedition! First, the bag would have to be thoughtfully packed with enough nappies for the boys and panties for my daughter. Then the bibs, as both boys would always throw their milk back up at some point, and of course, pacifiers. If I left home without their favorite ones, God help me, the whole supermarket would know! The double buggy was as wide as a door. A skateboard was attached to the back under the bars for my daughter to stand on.

The Paintbrush

Forget sleeping at night! Sleep, what was sleep? I didn't have that for many years to come. The boys slept together in their own cribs in the same room. I would rock one to sleep, then I would sleep on the carpet between them to make sure one of them didn't wake the other one up. This went on for 18 months.

James had terrible colic. Sometimes, at 2 am, Jonathan would have to take James in the car and drive him around the neighborhood to get him to sleep.

Life was fast and full. I loved it most of the time, but I still had moments where I felt out of control, especially when I had gone without sleep for several days. I was no longer caught up in the pattern of anorexia and bulimia as a way of trying to control my life. I shifted gears, and control began showing up in how I managed my household and family.

As a result of my dyslexia, I needed to convince myself that I had everything under control. Today, I understand that was an impossible expectation I put myself under, yet it was part of my journey. Dyslexia pushed me to believe I had to overcompensate and that everything had to be perfect so that no one would judge me for not being perfect myself.

Fresh food was an essential part of keeping my family healthy, so I made home-cooked meals from scratch every night. As a pastry chef, I baked fresh bread and cakes every Thursday, preparing for our Friday Shabbat dinner. And in between all of this, as if that wasn't enough, I still made all the novelty cakes for my friend's children's birthdays.

We lived in a small Jewish community with high expectations. Everyone looked at what you had and what you did. I didn't want to be judged that our home was messy or untidy when someone visited. For me, this reflected a

5 | Growing Into Me

cluttered, disorganized mind, which dyslexic people try so hard to compensate for. I later learned that until I dealt with these root problems, they would continue to show up in my life in different ways. Being a SuperMum was my job and my identity. No one could do it better than me. I had it all under control at all times. At least, I believed I did.

Time for Me to Meet Tia

Around the time Joshua was born, we were blessed to have the financial ability to buy a lovely house in a beautiful neighborhood. But the house needed some interior work, so we went to live with my in-laws until it was finished. After three months, we finally moved in.

One day, I made a call to a drapery designer named Marisol, whom a good friend of mine had introduced me to. I loved my friend's curtains and felt Marisol would be the perfect person to help me with ours. On the day we met, we felt an instant and deep connection.

In the midst of our first conversation about fabric choices, I broke down crying, and she asked me what was wrong.

"I am so tired. Everything feels so overwhelming. I feel like I am on the verge of a nervous breakdown." At that moment, I didn't feel I had the head to think about designing draperies even though I knew I wanted to. My Octopus SuperMum syndrome was finally getting the better of me. It was one of the first times in my life I let my guard down, showing my vulnerability and exposing my imperfections to a stranger.

I sat there trying to look at the fabric samples and crying uncontrollably. Finally, Marisol was so kind, putting her arms around me. She said, "Maybe you just put yourself under a lot of pressure and just needed someone to talk to today."

She was right. We continued chatting, and I shared some past trauma I believed had already healed. I told her about the inner voice that had guided me since I was young. She started talking about spirituality, and what she shared sparked an interest within me. It felt right as I listened intently. We spent four hours together and never even got to the drapery part.

As we talked, she suddenly looked at me strangely and asked, "Is Tracey your real birth name?" Then she said, "Because you don't look like Tracey to me."

"I never felt that I looked like Tracey either," I agreed.

She sat intently staring at me for a while, then said, "Tia—that's what you look like to me!"

Without any hesitation, at that very moment, that name felt so right to me! "Yes," I said. And so, on that day, Tia was born.

Spiritual Seance

A few weeks went by. Then, one afternoon Marisol called me and told me I had been on her mind and invited me to the spiritual seance she mentioned when we first met.

Although connecting with my inner voice was my usual, everyday way of life, I had never gone outside myself to do anything like a seance. "Why not?" I said, "Yes, I would love to!"

Picture the scene. I am sitting in a comfortable dining room chair in the living room of the leader's home in a circle surrounded by 12 other people. The leader is sitting to my left, and Marisol is seated to my right. I am listening to the leader chatting with the other attendees when I hear a voice I had never heard before say, *Tell him we're ready.* I ignored the voice, not realizing it was being spoken to me. Then, again, the voice said, *Tell him we're ready.* I looked around the room to see if someone was standing behind me and realized the voice I had heard was coming from a space outside of me.

I didn't want to look stupid and hesitated. "Excuse me," I finally said to the leader. "Something really strange is happening to me. I heard an unfamiliar voice telling me to tell you that they were ready to talk. It's not coming from me. I don't know quite what to make of this."

He didn't seem very happy to hear what I was saying, clearing his throat, he said, "Quiet everyone!" Then he quickly started the seance. First, he told us to close our eyes and call in our spirit guides and loved ones.

Within a very short time, I was drawn into a deep meditative state. I had not experienced this before. Suddenly, I heard a woman scream, "Close the circle down! She has darkness around her!"

I opened my eyes in shock and saw a woman on the other side of the circle pointing straight at me. Oh my God, what was this lady seeing around me? Was I finally being exposed to all the negative things I felt about myself? I jumped out of my seat, looked at Marisol, and ran straight out the front door.

Marisol came running after me and found me crying and running around like a lunatic on the grass. In uncontrollable sobs and tears, I said to Marisol, "You see? I knew it. I knew I was having a nervous breakdown. That's what she must be seeing when she said I had darkness around me! What else can it mean? What do you think she can see?"

The Paintbrush

I was beside myself, crying and pacing the grass like a mad woman back and forth.

The next thing I knew, Marisol was on the phone with a friend, and I heard her explaining what we had just experienced and what that woman said about me. After she hung up, she said, "Tomorrow, we will meet my friend Derek." He has told me to tell you he will explain everything to you then.

This was the second time I'd met Marisol, and I didn't know her well. She could have been a psychopath for all I knew. One minute we are in a seance; next, I am running around like a madwoman shaking off the darkness. Now, she has arranged for me to meet someone else whom I didn't even know.

But the maddest part of all of this was, somehow, I trusted her.

White Cloud

The following day, we both went to meet Derek, the psychic. Unfortunately, Derek did not live in one of the safest areas in south London. I met Marisol at the train station near my home. The night before, she had specifically instructed me to not put any makeup on, not to wear any jewelry, and to dress understated as this was an area where a few stabbings had already made headlines in the news.

We got off at Tooting Bec train station around noon and walked a few streets to his house. We had to look for the correct number because there were 15 homes in a row connected to each other, and all of them looked alike.

We knocked on the door, and a woman answered it and invited us in. As we walked through the front door, I could

5 | Growing Into Me

hardly see what was inside amidst the cloud of cigarette smoke. She kindly guided us into the living room, where Derek was waiting for us. He completely filled up a large armchair, his belly protruded between his suspenders and over his belt, and a lit cigarette rested on an overflowing ashtray on the table next to him. He looked about 65 years old but could have been much older.

Marisol and I sat on the dark velvet sofa, trying to ignore the dog hair. I looked around the room and noticed that all the curtains were drawn—the front and back windows too. And the one door we had walked in through was the only door out. So, I scooted a little closer to Marisol on the sofa.

Derek introduced himself to me and said, "Welcome. I have known for years that you were coming. My guides told me that one day I would meet you. I have a message for you from your main spirit guide."

The next thing I knew, he went into a trance state, and a Native American Indian called White Cloud introduced himself and said to me, "Your light is powerful, and not only are you holding the energy for planet Earth, but you are also holding the energy for other dimensional frequencies too. Your light is very bright, and just like a moth attracted to the light, those who need light will be attracted to yours."

While listening, I looked at Marisol in total shock and whispered, "Who have you brought me to? Who is this man? Is he all there? Who and what is White Cloud?"

Derek carried on channeling White Cloud and said, "At the seance, the woman screamed because she was seeing her darkness in the reflection of your light. Your thoughts about having a nervous breakdown were because your emotional human self has been absorbing the pain of others on a global and personal level for years. You are way too open. You need to learn how to shield yourself. You were never born to be like others. It is time to let go of this illusion and what you believe is expected of you. Of whom you think you are supposed to be and how you are supposed to live. It is time for all this to change."

I sat there with my jaw open and eyes wide as if I were a deer in headlights. A regular, everyday woman who had never experienced anything outside her inner voice, suddenly witnessing Derek transform into a large Indian chief shocked me. His facial features changed, and I saw White Cloud in Derek's face.

White Cloud then looked at both Marisol and me and told us that we were his granddaughters in another lifetime when he was Chief Joseph of the Nez Perce tribe.

Marisol was as surprised as me! No wonder we had an instant connection to each other! We were sisters from another lifetime.

At this point, Derek stopped channeling White Cloud, and I started to shake. I could feel myself entering a trance state, and for more than two hours, the energy of White Cloud started communicating through me to Derek.

Now Marisol's jaw was hanging open, watching me channeling. She knew then why she had felt compelled to bring me to Derek.

Afterward, Derek said, "This is what you were born to do. This is why you came. I will teach you how to channel and hold White Cloud's energy and the other energies you will connect with later in life."

5 | Growing Into Me

It wasn't long before I became a trance medium, but it took me a while to trust my abilities to channel White Cloud. Once I did, all these profound messages started pouring out of me. Derek taught me how to protect my physical and emotional body and hold my light strong while channeling. He was very strict about this. He taught me this was the most important lesson when working with other dimensions.

Mediumship Mentoring

For the next several years, Marisol and I would meet with Derek weekly at my home. I learned how to embody the energy of White Cloud and the frequency of different energies. I was taught how to call them all in. I had to be very strict with how I was in command of what I was allowing myself to experience. These different energies were not in control of me; I was in control of them. I learned to discern what felt safe to me and what did not.

During one of our sessions together, I shared with Derek a recurring dream of seeing monsters behind doors that I was terrified to walk through. In an exercise, he helped me open each one of them. I understood those doors were based on my fears, painful experiences, and people who had hurt me.

Reflecting on this synchronicity, I know that there are no coincidences. Every experience we have is meant to be. Even when we feel emotionally broken and mentally and physically overwhelmed, there is always a bigger picture just out of sight.

The monsters behind the doors were my old false beliefs about dyslexia, being stupid, lazy, bulimic, and the failing of my first marriage. Derek got me to walk through each door, one by one. As I did this, the hold the traumas had on me started to release. Trauma has many layers. I had already peeled back the first few layers after my divorce—now it was time to go deeper. It would take a few more years before I would finally heal them for good.

Interior Designers to Ya-Ya Sisters

Around this time, Marisol and I decided to go into business together and open an interior design company. I loved her work ethic. I had a good eye for design, so we became business partners. We named our company and showroom The House of Escarabia.

We were interior designers by day and spiritual Ya-Ya teachers at night for nearly ten years. Once a month, Marisol and I would hold classes to help people develop their own spiritual awareness. We taught them to trust and feel comfortable receiving their messages and claiming their strength and inner wisdom. The ladies looked forward to coming to our monthly meetings. They felt validated; their emotional selves felt nourished, appreciated, and loved. These sacred meetings were so heartfelt and inspiring.

Precious Souls

It was also during this time that I began to understand my gifts more. One day in a meditative state, I was guided to a beautiful garden full of the most exquisite, colorful flowers. Everything, including the grass, the animals, the trees, and the sky, were all vibrant and alive with life force.

5 | Growing Into Me

Walking in the garden, I was guided to a small white outbuilding surrounded by beautiful trees. Even the roof was pure white, it felt so serene and full of peace. I followed the path to the front door and opened it. As I entered the room, I saw all these children playing happily. Suddenly some of the children saw me, shrieked with joy, and ran up to me. They hugged me, saying, "We knew you were coming!" These precious souls were in transition. And so, every day for about a year, I would put myself into a deep meditative trance state so that I could go and visit with the children. This lasted about 20 minutes. Every time I visited, it was beautiful to witness the light around them becoming stronger and brighter. I believed I was helping them transition from the separation of their human self into the light frequency they were transitioning back into.

One day I returned to find that the room was empty; they had all left. I asked my inner self, *why?* And I heard, *it was their time, and now your next lesson would be elsewhere.* This is how it was for me—deeply profound and truly magical.

Sharing the Gifts with My Family

I enjoyed my spiritual classes and would often tell Jonathan and the kids about some of the things that I was learning. After our weekly class, Derek and Marisol would both stay for dinner. My family got to know Derek so well that our kids called him Uncle Derek.

During one of my earlier lessons in channeling with Derek, White Cloud gave my children their spiritual names. Melissa is the Sun who Rises. James is Earth Walker. Joshua is

Glow in the Light. Jonathan loved to joke and named himself He Who Blows Wind!

This was how my beautiful family embraced all that I was doing. Never once did they think I was crazy! Nutty, yes. But crazy no.

On full moons, Jonathan, Marisol, the children, and I would hold a howling to the moon party at the bottom of the garden with our friends the gnomes, and fairies.

Around the house, we had an abundance of crystals and as little children they loved them! I would teach them the energy that each one held and how to use them when they had tummy aches, headaches, and other ailments. On exam days, I would help them choose a crystal to carry in their pockets to school. Melissa, James, and Joshua each had a collection of crystals in their rooms and to this day crystals, are a big part of the decoration in their homes.

Meeting Mother Meera

Over time, Marisol and I met some very powerful teachers. Mother Meera, the embodiment of the Divine Mother, was one of them. Marisol knew I needed healing and said, "She's a wonderful healer, I am going to Mother Meera, and you're coming with me." We traveled to Germany to sit in Darshan with her.

Mother Meera is honored by her devotees and seen as the embodiment of the Divine Mother.

5 | Growing Into Me

What is Darshan

In total silence, we sat with 500 people in a large room for two hours. Then, one by one, everybody in the room kneels in front of Mother Meera to receive the sacred blessing of Darshan.

I remember sitting in my chair, waiting for my turn to sit in front of her. Unsure of what to do, I whispered to Marisol, "How will I know when I need to go to her?"

"You'll just know," she replied.

As I sat there, I experienced a deep presence of serenity and peace. About an hour later, I felt my body levitate off the chair. In my wildest dreams, and, believe me, I was having plenty of them at that time, never had I experienced anything like this before. I went and knelt in front of Mother Meera.

She held my head in her hands and looked directly into my eyes. It was as if she was looking into my soul and filling me with light. I felt the most beautiful, loving exchange of energy and a powerful presence in me, rearranging my thoughts and recalibrating my frequency.

Marisol and I both received deep clearing and healing of our bodies. But unfortunately, it brought up so much toxic emotional energy that when we returned home, we both had severe flu and were laid up in bed for two weeks. When we recovered, we felt like our insides had been polished.

Over the years, I have sat in Darshan with Mother Meera, and I even had the privilege of assisting her team once in Florida when she came. It was such an honor to be a volunteer.

The Paintbrush

Years later, one day, I received an email from one of the ladies I had met at the Florida Darshan. She told me that I had impacted her life by what I had said at the time and that she had a gift she wanted to send to me.

A few weeks later, I received a massive box in the mail. It was a beautiful 24" painting of Mother Meera that still hangs in my home to this day.

Mother Meera's energy is a big part of my life.

One of my favorite quotes of hers reminds me at times in my life when I need to hear it the most, that I am never on my own, that I am one with God wherever I am.

When you know you are one with God, you are free to become yourself, individual and holy.

Mother Meera.

Tia - Maria Girls in Madrid

Over the years, Marisol and I would go on buying trips together for our interior design company. Even furniture expos would transition into a spiritual experience. Individually, we were powerful. Together, our energies were electrifying. We'd walk arm in arm, and the suppliers would say, "There they are, the Tia Maria girls. Just give them what they want!"

One such trip stands out in particular—our trip to Madrid. Arriving two days early, Marisol and I decided to go to a park for a Sunday afternoon stroll. As we entered the park, we saw all these healers set up around the perimeter of the grass, working in different modalities.

We watched one person offering a healing session—he was walking on their backs and banging the bejeezus out of them. Marisol and I were shocked; we had never seen a healing session like that before. Then, we saw this tiny, frail, 80-year-old lady wearing all black waiting as she was next in line.

We both looked at each other, and I said to Marisol, "If that happens to this little old lady, he'll break every bone in her body!"

Marisol went up to the old lady and spoke to her in Spanish. She told her that we were healers and that we would love to give her healing if she needed one. The woman agreed and looked very relieved. Marisol called me over, and the next thing I knew, we were both lifting this frail little woman off the ground because she could hardly walk. We helped her to a tree where we sat her down to do the healing on her. I went into a trance and called in White Cloud. Marisol also connected with his energy and facilitated transformational healing through us. I never ask White Cloud or the person I'm facilitating healing about their issue. I don't feel I need to know. If it is important, then I'm told. I just let myself be the pure channel and trust that the Divine Source knows precisely what to do.

As soon as we finished facilitating the healing, the old lady got up, stood up straight, and like a jumping jellybean full of energy, repeatedly kissed and hugged us. Then, she walked across the grass and was gone. It was the most profound healing experience ever. That evening we both shared a toast to White Cloud and the divine light over a glass of wine.

What an amazing miracle we had witnessed!

Train to Toledo You Hope!

The next day, as we still had time to have fun and explore before our exhibition started, Marisol said, "Do you want to go on an adventure to a beautiful fortress town outside of Madrid called Toledo? You will love it!"

I replied, "That sounds fabulous, let's do it."

We got to the train station and bought our tickets. The train wasn't leaving for an hour so off I went to get some espressos for us both.

Within a few minutes, Marisol came frantically running into the coffee shop and said, "Quick, quick, the train is leaving now!"

I said, "But it can't be leaving; it is supposed to be leaving in an hour. It can't be the right train."

"Yes, yes, it's the right train."

She was always bossy, so I said, "Okay, Mari." I followed her out, even though my gut feeling was telling me this was not the right train. We jumped on board and quickly realized there was nowhere for us to sit as we saw each seat was numbered, and our tickets didn't have a seat number on them.

I followed her as we walked to the back of the carriage to find somewhere to sit. The conductor came along ten minutes into the journey, validating all the tickets. He came to us, and I could see Marisol's facial expression slowly plummeting as she stood up and made me stand up too.

I asked her, "Where are we going?" She said, "Well, I've got some news for you. You are right. This train is not going to Toledo."

"How interesting," I said with a big smile on my face. "So, where is this train going?"

"Alicante," she replied!

Hmmm. "How far is that?" I asked.

"Four hours," she replied.

So that would be an eight-hour round trip. It would be 12 am in the morning by the time we got home, and, to

5 | Growing Into Me

add salt to the wound, this was a non-stop train, where the only place we could sit was at the bar. So, I laughingly said to myself, *there was going to be a lot of drinking going on for eight hours.*

Not five minutes into our journey on our non-stop train, it suddenly stopped, and the doors opened. We looked at each other, grabbed our bags, and jumped off the train with shrieks of laughter to find we were in Toledo. That was the magic we created together. Wherever we went, we were larger than life.

Attracting Goodness

This time in my life was one of the most alive and happiest times—my family was thriving, my kids were growing fast, my husband and I were happy, and my partnership with Marisol was a big part of my everyday life. In fact, my kids felt they had two mums as Marisol spent a lot of time with us as a family, and so did her two teenage children, Stuart and Joanna.

Marisol and I, to this day, are two halves of one whole. Our energy together amplifies everything that is love. That is why strangers would feel comfortable, alive, and safe whenever they met us. It was our energy that they were attracted to.

Every year Marisol and I would go on an annual buying trip. These trips were so much fun. I would take off the Octopus SuperMum hat for a little while, and I would get to dress up in high heels and become a sophisticated interior designer.

On one furniture buying trip to Valencia, we had brought our company's brand-new Canon camera to take pictures of the latest materials and textile designs we hoped we would see.

The Paintbrush

We always liked to arrive at least one or two days before any exhibition started so we could explore a little.

The first morning after arriving, we decided to sit outside and have breakfast at a little coffee shop. Marisol went inside to get us coffee and by the time she returned, the camera had been stolen. I didn't see anything or anyone. It happened in the blink of an eye. We were both devastated. We decided to go to the police station to report it and started off walking arm in arm.

Suddenly, out of nowhere, this man appeared and introduced himself as Paco. Marisol started talking to him in Spanish. The next thing I knew, he invited us to link arms, Marisol on his right and me on his left, as he escorted us to the police station. On the way, Paco shared in his broken English all the beautiful buildings we were passing and about the history of Valencia. After walking for about an hour, he kindly delivered us to the police station, where we were able to report the camera being stolen. We thanked Paco for his help and guidance and said our goodbyes.

A little while later we decided to take a taxi. The driver's name was Juan and he was very talkative. Within a few moments he began telling us that he had rewritten the Bible and sent a copy to the Vatican and was waiting to hear back from the Pope. That evening he invited us to his house for dinner to meet his family! We attracted goodness wherever we went, which became normal for us.

Strangers would come up to us and offer help. They would invite us for dinner and just give us things. But maybe we were not strangers after all, and this is how the world was designed to be—full of kind, open-hearted souls caring about each other.

5 | Growing Into Me

Angels Around Me

One experience I will never forget happened on my way to work one day. Naughty me was driving without a seatbelt on a fast highway when I heard my inner voice say, *Put your seatbelt on! You will have an accident, but you will be okay!* I immediately listened and put it on.

As I turned off the road, I remember saying to myself, *I didn't have an accident. I must have imagined what I heard.* Suddenly, out of the corner of my eye, I saw a 60-ton truck carrying diesel take the corner of the road too quickly as if it was doing a movie stunt. The truck then flipped over and slid sideways straight into my car. My car was pushed to the edge of a grass slope and was hanging off. If the balance had tipped ever so slightly, my car would have slid further down and crushed the back in, too. Diesel fuel spilled everywhere. The front of my Mercedes was completely crushed up to my steering wheel. It's incredible that the airbag never even went off. I felt a surreal feeling around me, a presence of calmness, and a sense that a forcefield of light was inside the car with me. It took the rescue team an hour to cut me out of the vehicle.

Thank God I listened to my inner voice that day, and I *trusted* what I heard. It was a true miracle that I got out of the car alive. I had severe whiplash but thanked God I was all right. Again, a team of angels was with me.

From that day onwards, I never again drove without my seatbelt on.

The Paintbrush

Learning to Have Faith and Trust

Marisol had recommended I visit an excellent psychic that she had seen, so I did.

During our reading, the first thing she told me was, "I wouldn't want to have your life purpose." I asked why and she responded, "You are here to assist in clearing the Karma of the planet."

I half-jokingly asked, "Can I change my mind?"

She smiled and said, "No." Then she continued, "I see you taking a trip abroad on your own to learn something."

I asked, "Will I be going with someone else?"

"No, I don't see anyone else around you, just you on your own."

I felt overwhelmed when I came out of this intense reading. My thoughts were racing, *Karma of the planet? A trip alone? To learn something?* I felt so confused. I assumed a trip and learning had to do with my business, as I never traveled anywhere business-related without Marisol. And any other type of travel I ever did was with Jonathan and the kids. Never alone.

In theory, it might have looked like I was an independent woman. But I lived a very protected urban bubble way of life. Everything was taken care of for me, including putting gas in my car each week. So, traveling on my own was never going to happen.

I called Marisol and told her about the reading. I made her promise me that no matter what, nothing would ever pull us apart.

I thought about the reading for weeks. I had a strange feeling about it. Try as I may, I couldn't shrug off the feeling of worry.

5 | Growing Into Me

In my mind, I played over and over again what I had heard. I just couldn't understand what the reading meant by going on a trip on my own to learn. To learn what? I kept looking for signs. There were times I wished I'd never gone to see the psychic.

I had done so much spiritual work on myself through the many layers of trauma, worry, and fear. Yet there I was, caught up in it all once more.

In my mind, I was creating something that hadn't even happened yet. My old programming of self-doubt resurfaced once again. I was confused, and the problem with confusion is it separates you from your inner knowing. I would ask my inner voice to help me understand what was coming, but I kept hearing that I had nothing to worry about. I knew this was true, but still, I couldn't stop myself from worrying. I felt so confused. I knew in one breath that I had the power to override the worry. This is what I had been taught by White Cloud in my spiritual development classes. Yet my ego just kept overriding my soul.

I was caught up in a cycle of disconnection from my inner knowing.

I've learned that when someone predicts something in your future that you are not ready to experience or even understand, this creates a detrimental disconnection to your well-being. It can play havoc on your mind.

My thoughts were running into the future. Logically I knew this! I knew I had not taken the necessary steps to get there. But as far as I was concerned, I was already there. I was caught up in fear, not faith.

When you go through life worrying about the future, you give your power away to the fear and to the unknown.

The Paintbrush

This is fight or flight. I was caught up in flight mode. I wasn't in the moment. I was in the past and in the future. These are dangerous places to be in all at once. Together they rob you of your joy and your inner peace.

The more you learn to trust and stay present in the moment, the calmer you become, and the clearer your mind becomes too.

Only when you quiet your mind and stay present in the moment can you hear and trust what your inner voice is saying to you. This state of awareness is so powerful that it brings you into a calmer space within yourself where your mind and emotions connect in balance. This then turns fear into faith.

I call this the Intuitive Mind Space, which I teach at my BeWellness retreats.

Only by training our minds to be still and listen can we hear clearly.

And so, my friends, in the next chapter, you will read about a significant turning point in my life that would test my faith and trust on every level. This was the start of yet another life-changing lesson.

5 | Growing Into Me

Reflection of Wisdom

Time,
time,
time.
It is now that time!

Time to awaken
dear one.
Step by step
you go.
Your adventure
awaits.

6
Time to Be Broken Open

The Tide Turned

One day, just like that, the tide turned.

Jonathan and I had been subsidizing the high rent for our interior design showroom out of our own funds. When the rent dramatically increased, he decided we couldn't do it anymore, so we had to close our doors. Both Marisol and I knew it was the right thing to do–it was our only option–but still we were devastated. After 10 years together, we both went in different directions. The abrupt end of our business put a wedge between us for a while. She carried on the drapery side of the business, and I returned to being a stay-at-home mum.

Someone Show Me the Way

They say that to have a happy life, you have to look at it like a pie. Half is for your spouse and kids, and the other half is filled with things that nourish you: hobbies, sisterhood friendships, retreats on your own, self-awareness classes, and times of introspection. What I came to understand was that the relationship between Marisol and me made up the entire half of my pie. With that gone, my mask of illusion was placed back on my face again. There was a painful, massive gap in my heart and soul. Every day I had to pretend I wasn't suffering, but I was.

The nervous breakdown I thought I was having at 30 was now happening at 40. I remember walking into a supermarket one day and thought I would have a panic attack. I stood in front of the display of produce and couldn't breathe. I couldn't even choose which type of lettuce to buy. My brain couldn't take any more of the emotional roller coaster I was on.

So, it switched off.

From January to June, I received no messages from my inner voice or my Divine Being. Nothing was guiding me. My inner world was radio silent.

Every morning, I would get dressed, put my makeup on, put a smile on my face, take the kids to school, and chat in the playground with the parents—normal bubbly me. By the time I got home, exhausted from pretending, I would need to lie on the rug in front of the fireplace with my arms around my dog Jazzy and sleep. Sleeping during the day was what I had to do to keep going. I would call on my inner voice and my Divine Being, *please, show me the way!*

I heard nothing!

The Messenger & the Message

Until June 24th, around 4 am in the morning, my Divine Being woke me up and said, *Tomorrow morning, go online and look up 'Meditation in Italy.'* At that very moment, I knew that something powerful had changed. After 6 months of silence, I had finally received a message and felt connected again to my divine self.

I took my kids to school that morning and then raced home. I typed into the computer, "Meditation in Italy." This brought up Assisi. I sat back in my chair and thought, *Assisi… Italy?* I went back in time and saw myself as a sad 10-year-old sitting in the chapel, seeing the beautiful beam of light coming through the stained-glass windows and hearing the message, *don't give up. You will understand more by the time you are 40 years old, this we promise.* I was now 40 years old, and I knew then that I had to go to Italy—something in Assisi was calling me to go. I realized the time had come. This was the journey I was to take on my own.

I called Jonathan at work and told him about the message I received from my Divine Being. He could hear the joy in my voice and knew something was different and said, "If you need to go to Italy, go, I'll take care of the kids. I've got you covered." This was a massive undertaking because Melissa and the boys went to different schools, and their school days were full of activities. At dinner that night, we told the kids. They said, "If you feel the need to go, then you must go, Mum. We'll be fine."

For six months, I had been lost in deep sadness. I felt guilty for not being there for my family. Octopus SuperMum had no strength left in her tentacles. I didn't know who I was anymore. I knew who I was on my spiritual level, as a wife and mother, but beyond that, who was I?

It was time to figure that out. I knew I wanted to be a wise, enlightened human being. I wanted to give my children the best of me so they could be the best versions of themselves. But first, I had to know what that meant for myself.

The Paintbrush

The message I was given from the psychic that day, "You will go on a journey to learn something," became clearer. No matter how much I felt I had learned, now was the time to learn more and take that journey she spoke about on my own.

To prepare me to travel to Italy, I contacted a company called Simple Peace Retreats Assisi online, run by a couple named Bruce and Ruth. Having never traveled alone before, I needed to feel safe. Ruth and Bruce recommended a hotel for me to stay in. This gave me the courage in my mind to go.

Taking One Step at a Time

At 8 am on the 28th of June 2004, I left for Assisi, Italy. I really believed I was traveling light until I tried to lift the bag. Next time, I remember saying, I am just packing my panties and nothing more. Sitting in a taxi on the way to the airport, I remember looking back towards my home, feeling an overwhelming emotion in my heart. I was leaving my world behind me, my husband, my children, and my comfort zone for the first time in my life. I wrote this in my journal,

I wonder if I will be the same person coming back. Am I nervous about making this journey? No, I'm excited and a little apprehensive. I know with all my heart that I'm walking the path of truth, and I am one with the light of love in the universe. My divine self and I are one, and as one, we are journeying together. Many blessings to us both.

I boarded the plane for Rome at London Heathrow airport and chose a seat. Sitting next to me were Wendy and David, a lovely couple from Northampton. We started chatting and in no time at all, it was time to land.

6 | Time to Be Broken Open

At Rome airport David, my first angel of the day, guided me to the bus that would take me to the train station for the next part of my journey. I remember thinking, *how beautiful; although we believe we are on our own, we're not really on our own at all. For every step we take, someone is sent to guide us.*

I looked for what I assumed would be an air-conditioned tourist coach bus. But instead, I saw a rickety-rackety old bus that looked at least 30 years old and very heavily traveled. I wondered how I would get my heavy bag onto the roof when I met my next two angels for the day.

I must have looked pretty distraught because suddenly, two beautiful girls from Australia said at the same time, "Are you alright, Lovie?"

I said, "Well, I'm not sure how to get my bag up there." Within a lickety-split minute, they picked up my heavy bag as if it was as light as a feather and effortlessly threw it into the luggage hold between the top of the bus and the chicken pen. The chickens were squawking like banshees.

As I stood there watching, I thought, *is this all we need to do—take one step at a time into blind faith and trust everything will be taken care of?*

As I boarded the bus, I saw that the seats were benches covered in pink velour, most of which were filled with three adults sitting shoulder to shoulder. I chose the only seat left, between a man and a woman. As I sat down, all I could feel through the thin worn-out velour covering were the springs, no cushioning for my poor toosh! The bus had no air conditioning, and a definite wafting of Eau de BO added to the experience! Here I was on a rickety bus crammed between people, and all I felt was alive and free!

The Paintbrush

Although I was in the rawest, most vulnerable place I had ever been, I knew in my heart that I was being guided to something that was my destiny.

Train to Assisi

The bus finally came to a stop, and I got off. Roma Termini is the largest train station in Italy and has over 800 trains departing daily.

I thought *I don't understand Italian. I wondered how I will find my way around what looked like Spaghetti Junction on speed!* With chickens still squawking, the two Aussie girls helped me again to get my bag off the roof. As I walked into the station, I took a deep breath and felt I would be guided to where I needed to go…and I was.

The fourth angel of the day, a kind Japanese lady, saw me looking around, trying to figure out what to do next. In broken English, she asked if I needed help. I nodded yes. And told her, "Assisi…train."

She said, "Come, come," and took my arm. She walked me to the end of a line and showed me where I could buy my train ticket to Assisi.

It felt so freeing to trust and to start letting go of control; I was amazed, miracle upon miracle, just like that was happening. Even though I was doing something so outside of my comfort zone, I knew I was being protected. I was being shown the way, every step that I took.

I was now seeing clearer. Although I had believed I was living my life in an expanded existence, I was not! I was actually living my life in a contained box of familiarity.

After buying my train ticket to Assisi, I purchased a yummy tuna mayonnaise baguette, sat on the ground with my back against a wall, and called Jonathan and the kids. "I made it!" I said, all excited. "I'm in Italy! I just got off a rickety bus and want to tell you about the miracles and the kind strangers who helped me along the way!"

They could already hear the difference in my voice, and all of them encouraged me to do what I needed to do! We all agreed that I would be on radio silence while I was in Assisi. They wanted me to immerse myself in the experience and not worry or micro-manage them. Unconditional love means without conditions. Today, this is the foundation my family is built on.

The next call was to my mum. God bless her! She had been concerned about me traveling on my own and was worried. Before I left, she told me to be careful, what to, and what not to do. As I sat against the wall munching on my tuna baguette, I told her about all the strangers I had met, my guardian, angels, and the experiences I had had so far, and told her not to worry.

My mum is a terrible worrier. A pattern I had inherited. I was starting to see my reflection in her behavior towards me taking the trip. I worried about my children, and she worried about me. I realized that worrying doesn't serve anyone. I was instilling in my kids the same inherited programming of worry, which, if I didn't change, could prevent them from claiming their power.

This realization was massive for me. It was showing me a huge part of my own growth. In a short time, I was starting to change my old patterns.

The Paintbrush

Happy Trekking

It was time to board the train for the next part of my journey. To get onto the train I had to jump over a huge gap that separated the train from the platform. I could see that if I missed it, I would fall right through and land on the track! So, I lifted my heavy bag and threw it with all my might onto the train. Then, I took a running leap to get over the gap and jumped aboard.

I found a seat, and once I got my breath back, I settled down and reflected on what it had taken me to get here—faith, courage, and trust to travel to a new country with a language I didn't speak. I took out my journal and wrote, *I am so grateful for the guidance and love that is surrounding me on my journey. My heart is full of gratitude. Will I be content to go back to life as it was?*

The end of the line was at the Foligno train station, which looked to me like an old deserted sleepy hollow town where I was to change trains. I lugged my bag off and looked around. While I was looking for the next train to Assisi, my arms and legs began shaking with anticipation as I struggled to read the signs written in Italian.

I deciphered the sign that said, Assisi Platform Four. The next thing was I had to figure out how to get there. Platform Four was across the tracks from where I stood on Platform Three. Picture this: the only way I could see to get to Platform Four was to climb down some steps on the side of the platform onto the train tracks, walk across three sets of tracks praying that no passing trains were coming, and climb up the steps to Platform Four onto the other side. All while lugging my heavy bag. And that is precisely what I did!

Talk about courage and determination to get across to the other side! Another new experience.

On Platform Four, I saw a little old lady sitting on a bench with a birds-eye view of the tracks I had just walked across. She was looking at me very bewildered as I climbed up. As I lugged my bag onto the platform, I laughed and thought, *how did she get here? Was there another way of getting across that I'd missed? Oh, boy, did I just walk the tracks for no reason? She must think I'm mad!*

Smiling at her, I said, "Hello."

"Hello," she said back, and the rest of her words were spoken in broken English. I smiled, pointed to myself, and said, "Assisi. Me, Tia."

She replied, "Santa Maria de Angelique," as she pointed to herself and said, "Maria." She took out her train ticket, pointed to a machine, and showed me how to validate mine with her hand movement. I validated my ticket, her train arrived, and we said goodbye.

A few minutes later, my train arrived, and I boarded it. I handed my ticket to the conductor; I was so grateful I had validated it because later I learned that had I not done that, I would have been fined 100 Euros.

Maria was my fifth angel of the day. I witnessed another miracle. Effortless and easy. Once more, just when I needed it, the universe sent someone to guide me on my way. I thought to myself, *what if our lives are constantly being guided, we just are not present enough to realize it?*

The Paintbrush

In my journal, I wrote this poem:

To the trekkers of the world
keep looking for your signs
some are on the ground
some are in the sky
but most are just in front of your nose.
Happy trekking this road called life.

Nine hours after leaving home, I was finally in Assisi. I made it! It was late at night. The tears of gratitude rolled down my face as I walked out of the train station. I was finally at the place I would call home for the next seven days.

Courage to Face Your Fears

My wish for you is this: Know that you will always be guided and that the first step is all you need to take. Know that courage lies within you. If I can do it, so can you. I learned that faith and inner peace go hand-in-hand, and both start with trust, one step, one day at a time—none of us know from one day to the next what the future holds. We wake up in the morning and experience a new day in our life. What a blessing. I guess that's why it is called the present! Living life is the present; it is the gift we get to open daily in deep reverence of gratitude and appreciation. On my journey alone to Assisi, I was starting to see this even more.

We mustn't fear growth; we mustn't fear change. Trust is a far easier and kinder emotion to live with than worry and fear. Learning to let go of them is the greatest gift we can experience for our emotional and mental selves. This is what this time in my life taught me. Staying small in my mind, staying safe, playing safe—this needed to change. You cannot grow if you allow yourself to be limited by old, out-of-date beliefs. So don't fear them. This was the time in my life when I was being guided to step into my own power and face my fears head-on. Assisi was the beginning of the next stage of my growth.

The Paintbrush

Reflection of Wisdom

*Face your fears and your fears no longer exist.
It takes a lifetime to live in fear,
but a second to conquer.
Once one fear is conquered,
many victories will follow.
For fear is the fear of fear itself.
We can achieve anything in life,
when fear is replaced
by calmness and trust,
by telling yourself you can do it,
and by taking the first hardest step,
the next and the next become easier.
And you become the conqueror.*

6 | Time to Be Broken Open

The Alchemist. There she is in her stage of deep transformation as she starts to burn through the illusions of old patterns and programs.

7
Roses and Love

The Attic Bedroom

The hotel I was recommended to stay in was situated in Assisi town, not too far from the Basilica of Saint Francis.

A very kind Italian man was waiting to check me in. He must have seen that I was exhausted because even though the hotel was not equipped for room service, he offered to make me something to eat after he helped me take my bag to my room.

Roberto was my sixth angel for the day.

The hotel consisted of three floors. Up and up, Roberto and I climbed. Three floors up, just when I thought we were finally at my room, he opened the door to another staircase. We went up until he finally delivered me and my bag to a room in the attic.

The ceiling was covered in beams, the highest point was in the middle, and the lowest was over my bed!

The full-sized bed was raised on a platform so that when I laid down and raised my arms, I could almost touch the

The Paintbrush

beams with my hands. My interior designer eye kicked in, and I thought, *who in the world designed this? What an interesting space!*

All I wanted to do was get into a hot shower. Well, the shower in my private 6 x 6' bathroom was not quite what I thought it would be. It must have originally been a cupboard converted into a wash your bits bathroom. Only inches from the toilet and sink, the shower had a hose hanging off the wall. It had a showerhead at the end and a drain on the floor for the water to run down. What an interesting room!

Roberto kindly made me a delicious sandwich and delivered it to my room. I sat on the bed, munching away, conscious of how close my head was to the ceiling. I am not always very good with new surroundings. Being sensitive to energy takes me a while at the best of times to settle in. I prayed as I looked around the room that I would have a really good night's sleep.

By the time I went to bed, it was around 1 am, and I was exhausted. By 5 am, I was still wide awake, tossing and turning, trying to get comfortable. Let's just say the bed was as hard as a board. In fact, a board would have been softer to sleep on!

Around 6 am, I went out onto the tiny Romeo and Juliet balcony of my room. The views were breathtaking! I could see all the way around the town of Assisi. I stretched my arms out and felt as if I was in heaven.

At 7 am, I was showered and ready for my magical day. It didn't take me too long to get dressed as I decided that for as long as I was in Assisi, I wouldn't put a lick of makeup on. It was time for the raw me to be seen.

7 | Roses and Love

Downstairs, on my way out, Roberto was at the desk just where I had left him the night before., I asked him if they had another room with a shower; lucky for me, they did. Bless Roberto. I prayed, *please, God let my bedroom have a proper shower, not just a hose!*

Child of the Rose

I had plans to meet with Bruce and Ruth – the people who facilitated meditation in Assisi later that day. But first, I wanted to spend some time in their spiritual center. I was eager to check it out.

The outside of the building looked very ordinary, but inside it was gorgeous with white stone walls and an ethereal light presence that invited me in. I instantly felt a sense of peace as I walked in.

Looking around, I was drawn to sit in front of a sacred shrine set into the white stone wall with a beautiful Divine Mother statue in it. Two ornate vases surrounded the statue on either side, filled with pink roses. I sat down on a floor cushion and meditated for a while.

Sitting in a deep serenity, I suddenly heard a voice within me say, *my divine child, put your head to the ground.*

So, I put my head on the cold stone floor. Again, the beautiful voice spoke, *from this day forward, you are a child of the rose. My voice is yours; your voice is mine. Let it be heard. I am you, you are me, and we are one together.*

I am now putting a halo of roses on your head; wherever you walk, you will walk with love and compassion in your soul and in your heart.

The Paintbrush

I knew in my heart, the beautiful presence speaking to me was the Divine Mother. She was the energy who placed a halo of pink roses on my head. The energy was tingling all the way through me and I felt that I was being illuminated with her light energy. It felt to me as if I had been initiated into the covenant of divine grace, light, and love.

Her mothering energy was so gentle and kind. I felt complete acceptance for the first time in my life. Her presence of unconditional love surrounded me as if she was giving my soul a huge hug. Love and compassion washed over me, and tears of joy poured down my face. The sweet scent of roses permeated the room. My heart began to open and fill up with a deeper sense of trust and acceptance. I felt as if I was being shown for the first time in my life that it was safe to be me and to be seen.

After this experience in the sacred space, I decided to go outside and explore a bit. So, I wandered around the town and found a local café where I had a delicious chicken salad for lunch. I sat in the shade, contemplating what had just happened to me. There was so much to take in.

Everywhere I looked, I saw roses and knew the Divine Mother was with me…even at lunch. The person sitting next to me at the café had a rose tattoo on her shoulder. They had roses on the table and rose and honey gelato on the menu.

Later that afternoon, I met Bruce and Ruth in their sacred space, where they welcomed me with open arms. We sat for a while next to the shrine of the Divine Mother enjoying a cup of tea. They both shared with me about their earlier calling to leave America and come to Assisi. I told them about my journey myself for the past 10 years and my spiritual journey of higher consciousness.

7 | Roses and Love

An hour later, people started arriving in their sacred space, and Ruth invited me to join them in a group meditation that Ruth led every day.

In the meditation, I connected with the Divine Mother once again. This time she took me on a beautiful journey, and I experienced a deeper consciousness of love. I saw myself as she did, as pure love. Through the Divine Mother, I could see the essence of my true beauty and the light that surrounded me. I thought about all the times I was unkind to myself and how I put myself under extreme pressure. When I saw how I had been treating myself, I wept tears of sadness.

I decided then it was time to release the need to be perfect. I felt as if layers and layers had already been stripped off me, literally peeled away. I was changing rapidly in a very short space of time. What was beginning to change was the program of the illusion that I believed was my truth.

In my journal, I wrote: *All there is, is love. And as we start to strip away old beliefs and patterns, we begin to clearly see the bigger picture of who we are and the miracle of life.*

The miracle of receiving the halo of roses that day was a symbol of divine love and the presence to me of my own transformation that was starting to happen.

After the meditation was over, I spent another hour talking with Bruce. We spoke about how we can sometimes feel confused, alone, and lost. I shared with him some of my past six months and the sadness I was holding on to. How it was part of a more powerful lesson, of learning how to love myself.

It takes a journey of tranquility, peace, and love to finally understand that the most precious gift of all is learning how to love ourselves. Most of the time, this is the hardest lesson of all to learn. We go around and around in circles, trying so

The Paintbrush

hard to change things in our outer world. Yet nothing will ever change until we connect with the beauty of our true selves. This usually only happens when something catastrophic pushes us toward change.

I left Bruce that afternoon deep in thought about everything we had chatted about. I walked, and I walked, and climbed higher and higher, feeling deep within myself this feeling of belonging.

Sitting in a leather wingback chair in a cozy coffee shop, I reflected on my profound day. I sat in silence, watching the world within the walls of Assisi go by. After a little while, I decided it was time to walk back to my hotel. It had been a long day.

Kaboom Assisi, Kaboom Tia

On the way to my hotel, I passed a hair salon and noticed a window sign saying, "Hair Braiding." Since I was a little girl, I dreamed of having my hair done in thin, tiny plaits. So, I went in to see if they could fit me in. Four hours later, the two ladies were standing in a pool of sweat after they had worked hard, plaiting every strand of my long thick hair. 40 teeny tiny braids later, each one was secured with a black elastic band.

As one of the ladies put the last band around the braid, one snapped and flew across the room just like that. Then, like something out of a Harry Potter scene, all the black elastic bands began to snap one by one, blowing off my hair and whizzing through the air. We all looked at each other in utter shock. As we watched them flying across the room, all the two ladies kept saying was, "Ooh la la la la!" and all I kept doing was laughing one moment and then saying ouch, as the bands painfully flicked my face!

I knew exactly why it was happening, though. No black bands for me. My time of mourning my old self was over. The energy of the Divine Mother did not want this for me anymore. Everything around me was to be light and bright. So, I chose the brightest colored rubber bands they had, and the poor ladies went about securing the 40 braids all over again.

When I told a friend this story, she said, "Your energy must have been so high! Thank God you didn't touch an electric plug because it might have been kaboom Assisi and kaboom you." We laughed.

That night I returned to the hotel and sat on the bed of my lovely 2nd-floor room with no beams touching my newly braided hair and wrote a profound channeled message from the Divine Mother. In this channeling, she explained the three layers of enlightened love.

Three Layers to Enlightened Love

A message from the Divine Mother

My child, when you tap into your divine energy and the power of your light, you awaken within your human self a deeper connection to what we call "enlightened love." Learning to love yourself is the first step.

There are three layers: the love of yourself, the love of another, and the collective love of humanity.

The Paintbrush

To simplify this, I will refer to it as me, you, we.
Layer One: Me.
Learning to love yourself.
Layer Two: You.
Only when you love yourself unconditionally and in complete totality will you attract someone who loves themselves in just the same way.

Nothing is broken. No one needs fixing. These two are fulfilled. They vibrate at a higher level of love.
Layer Three: We.
Together through this, they both create a powerful love that extends into the world. This is what we call enlightened love.

When I say love yourself, I am not referring to the singular self. No.

That's the problem. You tend to see yourself as just that! You: But you are far bigger than what you see.

What I am referring to as yourself is a collective of the divine self, your soul, and your human self. This is spirit, soul, and body as one. They are not separate individual parts. They are all one.

I know my child this message is deep and profound and has many layers to it. I am just planting a few seeds of wisdom as it is time for humanity to awaken to this knowledge.

I sat for a while digesting the message I had just channeled from the Divine Mother.

I knew from a very little girl that there was something in me that was far more significant than just my human self. My connection to my inner voice was one example. I knew my divine self pretty well, but it was the human, emotional part of me that I still had to master...*loving myself*.

7 | Roses and Love

Loving me was why I was brought on this journey to Assisi; to learn to love myself completely and unconditionally. As the Divine Mother had already said, *I am you, you are me, and we are one together.* Only when I connected with this love would I awaken a deeper connection with all that exists.

I was starting to understand the deeper meaning of the Divine Mother's channeled message to me. Loving myself was the first part of a much bigger picture. It wasn't just about me; it was about all of humanity, too. The me, you, and we are what we are here to create. It is the ultimate type of love. It is enlightened love. But first, I had to learn to unconditionally love *me*.

Me, Layer One

For a moment, I invite you to connect with the awareness of *enlightened love*. Connect with these three parts within you. The divine, the soul, and the human self.

For just a moment, see that you are connected to all three layers.

Close your eyes and take a breath. Feel the love and compassion of the Divine Mother as she guides you. *Hear her say, I am you, you are me, and we are one together.* For a moment, sit with whatever that means to you. There is no rush; take your time. Take another breath. Connect with the deeper layers of love within yourself.

Let the energy of this love expand within you and around you. Take your hands and put them on your heart as you feel the power of this enlightened love move through and around you.

The Paintbrush

Reflection of Wisdom

*Beyond the sun,
the moon,
and the stars
I am you
we are one.
Always and forever
we are.*

7 | Roses and Love

Enlightened Love. Me, You, We. I am one with all that is in the universe through time and space. Nothing is separate from me.

The Paintbrush

Blooming Flower. This painting reflects the abundance we have in our hearts. When the time is right, we awaken within us the essence of enlightenend love.

7 | Roses and Love

Energy in Motion. This painting reflects the power and frequency of energy that is always in motion, and is always working to bring us our highest good.

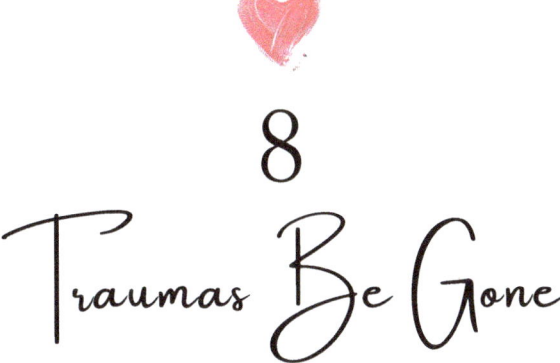

8
Traumas Be Gone

Layers of Stuck Trauma

The day after my hair braiding experience, I woke up with a high fever.

Only a day earlier, I had channeled that deep, profound message from the Divine Mother about loving myself, and here I was lying in a strange bed, in a strange place, feeling all alone. Being alone had always been a great fear of mine. I felt so vulnerable, lying there, unable to move my body due to the high fever. And no one to call. I certainly wasn't going to call Jonathan or my mum. I wouldn't want them to worry.

Throughout the day, I could feel my fever spike and was reminded of my childhood as a little girl when I often had tonsillitis. I already knew that my recurring tonsillitis signified that I had a blocked throat chakra then—this was due to me not feeling safe enough to speak my truth! I had done so much work on healing that part. Why now? And why in Assisi?

Crying, I called on the Divine Mother for guidance and help. I heard this, *It is time to release all that is stuck within you, the sadness, the judgment, the shame, and the guilt. You have*

The Paintbrush

held onto these emotions for far too long, and now through loving yourself unconditionally, you are to release them all. It is time.

It was time to let go of my old beliefs about myself that I had carried for far too long. Like old trash bags full of rotten stinky stuff—the abuse in my first marriage, the shame, and guilt I felt about my learning challenges, bulimia, anorexia, the loss of my business partnership—and those old beliefs about myself that were never true. It was time to let it all go, stop mourning what I wasn't, and start living what I was.

My Divine Source wanted me to release those layers of trauma I wasn't even aware I was still carrying.

Void of Energy

Again, I asked the Divine Mother to help me understand what I needed to know on a deeper level.

She said, *my child, Disease-ment - Disease is the disconnection from joy, happiness, and the ease of living in true abundance on all levels—when your thoughts don't align with your true state of well-being, you create within your mind, thoughts that contain judgment, pain, suffering, shame, and sadness. This then transfers into the body and settles somewhere where it will play havoc if it is not addressed. Ease is how every human being is meant to live every day, but unfortunately, this is not the case!*

As I heard this, I started to understand cause and effect better and how the dis-easement in my beliefs about myself showed up as tonsillitis in my childhood and how it carried on into adulthood.

The Divine Mother spoke as she explained what happens to unresolved trauma.

8 | Traumas Be Gone

The moment you experience any type of trauma, a void is created that has no energy. This closes down your natural state of well being. The energy around the trauma becomes black as it fills up with pain and sadness. These emotions stay stuck in a space where no light can reach it.

Then you try to get over the experience. Maybe you convince yourself that you have let it go and moved on. Or perhaps you pretend the trauma doesn't exist anymore and believe you are past it.

You leave it buried. Thinking that if it's forgotten, the trauma does not exist anymore. But it is not gone. You see, your body does not forget. Your body knows it's there. What was created in that space stays stuck and buried within you.

Then another trauma comes along, and another void is created where no light can reach it. Each layer of trauma fuels the other. It's a domino effect.

Over time, those traumas start to drain your true, natural state of well-being. Before you know it, you are in a space of diseasement.

When I heard this, I cried even harder. It made sense. I had put myself under all that unnecessary pressure, pain, and suffering. Lying there in bed, I knew I didn't want to waste one more day suffering. Now was the time to heal every one of those pockets of trauma. Again, I heard, *don't run away from your pain of the past; walk into it.*

I knew I had to travel into those dark places inside myself—those places full of sad memories—and heal them. I asked the Divine Mother to show me what I needed to do.

She said, *close your eyes, my child, and ask your body to show you how many layers of trauma you have.* I saw that I had

The Paintbrush

one in my stomach, another in my heart, and one still in my throat area. Then I heard, *imagine that you are connecting to that bigger part of you, the divine self, in everything that exists. Feel the love of this connection. Let it flood your whole body, with rays of light moving through you, pouring love into you. See the love blasting the spaces of darkness and watch as it transforms them all back into the light. Thank the trauma's, tell them that you are grateful and that now through gratitude, all that you feel is unconditional love.*

I did just that. I saw this beautiful light move through my body, spreading love and light through me. It was so powerful, so beautiful to feel my body start to respond.

Again, the Divine Mother spoke.

It is not necessary to know what the memory of the traumas are about. All that is important is for you to connect with your divine self. Sometimes knowing what the trauma is causes it to expand. All that you need to do is connect with the light. This raises your vibration and helps bring you back into a natural state of well-being.

Everything that I had been through for the past 40 years, I felt in my heart was being healed. Although I had done a lot of spiritual work on these traumas with Derek and White Cloud, this felt very different.

I drifted in and out of sleep and continued feeling the light of my Divine Being healing me.

It felt like I had a spiritual recalibration and that all the negative energy of those buried traumas was being replaced with light and a deep force of love.

Finally, the Divine Mother whispered in my ear, *Tomorrow, my child, you will be well.*

This message felt so kind and loving that I remember, with tears pouring down my face, saying aloud, "Yes, Divine Mother, I will be well." And as I carried on seeing my body infused with light, I knew that what I was experiencing was something so powerful, so divinely orchestrated, that tomorrow I would be well.

All through the night, I felt a team of angels surround me as if they, too, were helping my Divine Being infuse me with light. I remember waking up in a pool of sweat, as if the light inside of me was on fire like the alchemist, burning all the debris away.

And just like that, I woke up the following day, just as the beautiful Divine Mother had said, entirely well, as if I had never been sick. It was beyond a profound experience; it was a true miracle. I knew then that I had done it! I had let go of all the traumas. My body was full of light!

Easy Does It

I got out of bed as if a huge weight had been lifted from my physical body and my soul. I was raring to go. I felt lighter and brighter as I danced around the room. I felt the arms of the Divine Mother around me, rejoicing in the joy and happiness we were sharing together. I could feel how proud she was of me.

I heard her say, *Courage isn't given to the meekest of hearts. It is given to those who carry an intense light and who know that what they have gone through themselves, one day they will teach. You are nearly ready to teach my child.*

The Paintbrush

This powerful experience was another wondrous miracle. I knew deep within me that my soul was listening and agreeing. I had worked so hard to bring myself to this point in my life. Finally, my past was behind me, and I was walking forward free.

I took it easy the rest of that day, just going on short walks around the area, coming back to sleep and heal, still feeling the light moving through me, thanking my Divine Source for never giving up on me.

As it was a warm afternoon, I decided that I wanted to explore the town of Assisi and enjoy this newfound freedom in my heart. The sun was shining, the birds were chirping, and it felt as if my choir of angels was singing to me, *Hallelujah, she did it!* So, I decided to sit outside the hotel on a chair feeling the sun's warmth on my face and the gratitude in my heart.

I reflected on everything I had been through. I listened to the sounds around me. In just 24 hours, I had healed the traumas of the last 40 years. It is incredible what can happen in such a short space when you replace darkness with light. Miracles happen instantly!

Reflection of Wisdom

Give with your heart truthfully
And you will receive ten-fold
We are all rich people in the eyes of heaven
For we are all the children of God
Love is winning the lottery in life
To be able to walk, talk, and laugh with strangers
To enjoy silence
To hear the sound of the birds singing in the trees
This is wealth
And it is free
The greatest things in life are free
What we give, so shall we receive
And what we receive is love
So today just give a little love
And see what it brings

9
T For Tau

Hello Morning, My Dear Friend

It's time to explore. I planned to visit the Basilica of Saint Francis later that morning. I was beyond excited. But before doing so, I decided I would have breakfast in a lovely café not too far from the hotel that Roberto had recommended. With my journal in my hand and a skip in my step, I found the perfect table to sit at.

Another beautiful warm morning in Assisi. I watched as a young couple walked past me pushing a newborn baby in a stroller. They were beaming with happiness. My heart felt their love; I felt the surge of enlightened love they had for one another and their baby. Finally, I was starting to get it.

I decided to treat myself to the breakfast special. It consisted of freshly squeezed orange juice, hot fresh bread, homemade raspberry jam, crème fraîche, and a delicious apple fritter freshly fried only minutes before.

I love to watch people; it fascinates me. I can sit for hours doing just that.

The Paintbrush

After my second cup of coffee, I decided it was time to write some more thoughts about enlightened love. As I started to write, a lovely young girl sitting at the table next to me leaned over and asked if the apple fritter was worth breaking her diet. She could see from my plate that not even a crumb was left. Of course, I said to her definitely it was a must.

We started to chat, her name was Naomi, and she was from London, too. She was visiting her fiancé's sister. She couldn't have been older than 25 and had the loveliest long blond hair. She loved my braids and said maybe she would have that done to her hair.

Empathic Soul Energy Vampire

I'm not sure how we got onto the topic of empathic souls and energy vampires, but we did. She told me how sensitive she was, that she even felt drawn to me when she saw me. Naomi said that was why she chose to have breakfast at the café.

She said that her future sister-in-law, whom she was staying with, was very negative. All she did was complain about what wasn't working in her life. Naomi shared how drained she felt around her and how she was dredging going back to stay with her. She told me she was contemplating going home.

It was then that I placed the teacher hat on my head and shared some ideas to help her.

I said, "You may not realize this, but when you get caught up and absorb someone else's emotional energy, you give them

9 | T For Tau

your golden juju. Just like Dracula, they are drinking your life force from you. They are what I call energy vampires."

I then shared with her about a friend in London who had a difficult marriage. Every time I visited with her, she would tell me the same story over and over again. My heart would always want to lift her up, guide her and help her heal. But my inner being would remind me just to hold the space, listen and beam a loving light to her but I was to protect myself most of all, and not give any of my light, my energy away. I carried on explaining that my friend did not want to change anything; she just needed to purge her emotions. She was stuck in victim mode. And nothing I would say would change anything for her.

To make a difference in her life, all I needed to do was just be there for her and hold my light strong.

I told her that I had come to understand it was not my job to heal my friend or anyone else. All I could do was hold my light bright, keep it nourished and clear, keep my frequency strong, and beam my light, not give it away.

I told Naomi, "It is never that we are to use our own energy from ourselves—from our own reserves for another. It is for us to illuminate like a guiding light, as bright as a lighthouse so that others could find their own way too. Be the light in the world. Shine the way."

I then explained the Golden Fried Egg Rule that I practice every day.

The Paintbrush

Golden Fried Egg

The little gold specks in the white part are what I call munching vampires. Their desire is to get into our egg's golden part and drain it! That is a No! No! *Never can they be anywhere in the golden dome or the white of your fried egg.* If you feel drained, sad, confused, or angry, then be aware that one of those slippery suckers got in. Something is munching on your energy.

Clear them out by imagining a beautiful energy vacuum is removing them. Sucking those suckers up.

The yummy golden dome, the white of the egg that's all your real estate. No squatters are allowed.

The outer edge of the white part of the egg is where they get to hang out.

This keeps your energy field around you protected from getting drained by uninvited guests.

Naomi loved this visual idea and said, "I knew I needed to sit next to you today. I'm going to be very conscious of my fried egg and make sure no slippery suckers get into any part of it."

My heart felt so happy that, for just a little while, I was able to help enlighten a stranger. After everything I had shared with Naomi, she said, "I'm off to get my hair braided. You're such a wise lady, I want some of that wisdom on my head, too." I told her about the great salon down the street and added, "watch out for the black elastic bands; I recommend the colored ones." As she walked off, I smiled with a twinkle in my eye.

Peace and Enlightened Love

There is a presence of peace in Assisi that I have never experienced anywhere else in the world. It is as if everything is alive with love, gratitude, and acceptance. As I walked toward the Basilica of Saint Francis, I felt such a deep sense of beauty and warmth in my heart, knowing that something far bigger than myself was giving me a divine hug. I was still reflecting on my wonderful exchange with Naomi and how blessed I was to have a warm interaction with a stranger.

As I walked the streets, the people I saw had a lightness in their feet and a carefree way about them. But what I noticed the most was that everyone I saw was wearing a wooden T cross around their neck. I wanted to find out more about this T and what it meant. As I passed by a shop in the window, I saw a piece of wood embedded with sparkles carved in the shape of a T hanging from a leather cord with knots. It was calling my name.

Inside I found a lovely shop assistant who explained to me the significance and meaning of the wooden T. She said, "The T represented the word *tau*. It is the sign with which St. Francis of Assisi loved signing his letters. The symbol of

The Paintbrush

the Tau is sometimes considered to represent the habit of a friar with their arms stretched out. St. Francis is believed to have told his fellow friars that the habits they wore were in the shape of the Tau Cross. As such, they were to be walking crucifixes, representing the compassion and faithfulness of God. Tau crosses are often carved out of wood to signify humility, simplicity, and flexibility. It is the symbol worn by the Franciscan friars as a spiritual expression of love, peace, and joy for all of God's creations."

I immediately thought of T for transformation and my own journey from darkness to light that I had experienced the previous days.

"Her beloved Saint Francis," she told me, "took hold of the T as a symbolic reference to God. At the end of his life, Saint Francis became the living image of the *tau* he deeply loved, and that is why everyone wears in Assisi the T to this day in honor and devotion to their beloved saint and to God."

When she finished sharing the information with me, I felt great pride and love coming from her for Saint Francis and her faith. So, I decided to buy the T necklace I had seen in the window as a reminder of the love, gratitude, and transformation I was experiencing during my time in Assisi.

I left the shop and walked towards the Basilica of St Francis. At the entrance of the upper level of the Basilica carved into the grass, are the letters PAX which mean PEACE. As I entered the basilica, I saw banners with the word peace in every language: *shalom, salaam, paix.*

With tears in my eyes, I witnessed in this beautiful basilica the presence of oneness. What if oneness means seeing this world and the human race as one people under the sun? What if the universal religion was peace and enlightened love? Can you imagine living in a world like that? What if heaven is in our hearts, and we create heaven on Earth by living this way?

I continued walking around the basilica. Mesmerized by its beauty, and the exquisite frescos, I took my time studying how they created such beauty, and without any modern-day equipment. After a while I decided to sit down at the shrine of Mary Magdalene. I instantly felt this beautiful, kind presence surrounding me as I did. In the air, all I could smell was the sweetest of roses! It was as if I was being lovingly wrapped in a soft ethereal shroud. With my eyes closed, I saw the shroud made of translucent, iridescent material, beautiful and full of grace. My whole body felt as if it was being engulfed in the serenity and sweetness of pure love.

As I sat in this sacred space, I heard a beautiful feminine voice say, *sometimes you forget about yourself; sometimes life is so hectic that you forget to take time out. You forget about loving yourself. Today you are being reminded of this. Some of the most important gifts human beings can give to themselves are self-nourishment and taking time out to sit in reflection. This is not selfish; in fact, think of it as self-wishing.*

In my heart, I knew I was hearing this loving message from the woman Mary Magdalene herself, not the saint. It was as if she was a dear friend who was giving me some loving advice. The connection we shared at that moment was feminine to feminine, full of gratitude, appreciation, and love—pure, pure love. It was as if I was being gifted the essence and the grace to be myself, to walk forward with my heart full of joy.

I sat in this profoundly sacred experience for a while with tears of gratitude pouring down my face, not wanting to leave. Although the basilica was full of people, I felt as if there was no one there except us: myself and Mary Magdalene and the

The Paintbrush

beautiful energy of peace and enlightened love. I could feel a deep spiritual connection with Mary Magdalene and sat meditating in peace and quiet with her.

After a while, I pulled out a leaflet I had been given about the story of Saint Francis and started to read it. He was born around 1181-1182, His mother had named him John, after John the Baptist. However, his father, upon his return from traveling, changed his son's name to Francis. He wanted his son to have a more refined name, derived from France—the county where he believed his son would live one day.

In his early years, Francis lived a very privileged life. As a young boy, he loved to sing and was very learned. His father wanted him to become a businessman like himself and taught him all about French culture. At 19, Francis went into a battle between Assisi and Perugia. He was captured and taken prisoner. He was held in a dungeon for a year before his father paid the ransom for his release. It was during his imprisonment that Francis began to see visions from God. This changed his life. Upon his release, he decided to live a life of devotion, giving all of his money to the church. This made his father very angry, so Francis left his father's home and took a vow of poverty. In 1210, Saint Francis founded the Franciscan orders. This included two other orders: the Order of Saint Clare and Friars Minor. The Franciscan Order is one of the mendicant (vow of poverty) orders.

Saint Francis died on October 3, 1226, at 44, in Assisi, Italy. Today, he has a lasting resonance with millions of followers across the globe. He was canonized as a saint just two years after his death, on July 16, 1228, by his former protector, Pope Gregory IX. In 2013, Cardinal Jorge Mario Bergoglio chose to honor Saint Francis by taking his name and becoming Pope Francis. Many people do not know that in addition to being a Catholic Friar and Deacon, Saint Francis was also a mystic.

I finished reading the leaflet and felt more of an enlightened awareness about Francis the man, Francis the saint, the wooden T I had just bought, and the energy I was feeling at Mary Magdalene's shrine. I decided it was time to leave the basilica, to go outside to walk around the town and find something to eat for lunch.

Outside on a quiet side street, I found a local café and sat down to eat a delicious homemade sandwich. As I sat there, I felt drawn to write in my journal what I was feeling that day about the presence of peace and enlightened love and how I felt the rose was a reflection of this.

This is what I wrote:

The symbol of love is a presence that is felt and seen; it's in the eyes of the people I see walking around, in their smiles, and in their sharing; it's in every living thing! It isn't a word written or even spoken; it's more of an energy felt. Maybe I can describe how I see love as a rose!

Have you ever studied a rose?
Each rose has its own scent, its own look,
and its own color.
Each is unique.
Maybe this is what we are,
just in a different form.
We accept this so freely in a rose,
so let us accept this freely within each other.

The Paintbrush

Just for a moment, stop reading. If you can, please go and find a piece of paper and draw a rose. Remember, it doesn't have to be perfect! Color in your rose with love and appreciation for who you are and the life you are living. Don't rush this. Let this be a meditation, a connection to the love within you. It is important to take these moments during this next part of my book so that you, too, can feel the vibration and frequency of peace and enlightened love. That is my deepest wish for you.

When your drawing is finished, I want you to place your hand on your heart, breathe in love and let go of any of your thoughts and feelings that no longer serve you. See yourself as a rose—beautiful and full of loving grace.

After lunch, I wandered around the streets of Assisi, very much at peace and lost in my own thoughts. I studied the people I saw—how they embraced one another and carried on conversations as if they didn't have a care in the world. It was so wonderful to witness—beautiful smiling faces wherever I went. How amazing would it be if we as a world could see life this way through a different lens—maybe through the eyes of a rose, full of love, beauty, and oneness!

After another long, transforming day, I chose that night to have dinner in a quaint restaurant off a narrow, dark street. The significance of this? Another fear I let go of; I would never have walked down such a street in London, in the dark of night, on my own. I was changing rapidly.

The following day, I woke up with the sunrise, bright and early, feeling the energy of giving birth to my blooming awakened rose. I felt fearless, alive; I was bursting forth with the colors of happiness, excitement, and joy. I no longer felt like a dried-up weed, undernourished, and forgotten. I decided after breakfast to walk back down to the Basilica of Saint Francis. This time I wanted to sit at the shrine of my beloved Divine Mother.

As I sat down, I felt as if I was being cradled once more in the arms of this beautiful mothering energy in oneness and enlightened love. I sat with my eyes closed for a while, letting her transformational love wash over me again.

I heard the Divine Mother's voice say to me, *I want to talk to you about the You part of yourself within enlightened love.*

What is perfection, my child? Why have you strived all your life for this? This is part of the human need to achieve. This is an illusion. Nothing of need is true! When you let go of the need to be and do something, you open yourself up to the supreme miracles waiting to be gifted to you. Needing blocks your energy! Needing to be perfect comes from a lower vibration. This is not your truth. Your truth is to remember who You are! You are light, billions of particles of light. When you feel on an emotional level that you are in need, in lack, less than, you scatter your light, which creates separation, which leads you as a human being to feel less than worthy, and in need of proving who you are. Only when your light is intense can you truly see and know who You are—an enlightened supreme being. Whole. Not scattered. Within this awareness, you understand your human self and your light self. You are a powerful being of light, living the miracle of human existence.

When you put your human self down, you also put down your divine self and your soul self. This affects the entire universe. Mirror, mirror. What you believe about yourself is what you create. And what you create, you attract. From this knowing, be a wise mother to your children. Be conscious of how you speak to yourself, what you think about yourself and how you treat yourself. From

The Paintbrush

this place of wisdom, be the light and shine bright. Nothing else exists. Nothing else is true.

All that children need is enlightened love. enlightened love is the highest vibration; it collectively brings everything together: wisdom, trust, grace, peace, hope, tranquility, joy, gratitude, laughter, and so much more. Enlightened love is the anchor that gives any child the stability to grow emotionally and mentally strong. The rest they will find for themselves. When you let go of perfection, when you let go of control, you give a child permission to grow from a place of divinity. Loving yourself without judgment is the only love any mother can give to herself. The lighter you are about yourself, the easier it is for your children. Be the enlightened love, my child, be the enlightened love!

Such a profound message! In my striving to be perfect, I saw another layer of how much pressure I had been putting on myself: unrealistic goals, totally unhealthy to live by. It was time to soften the edges of my expectations and be kinder, gentler, and more loving to myself. I saw that my children were learning from me how to speak to themselves. Changing how I spoke to myself meant changing the pattern and breaking the illusion. I was expanding myself into a much higher frequency of collective consciousness, and by doing this, I was teaching them to do the same.

Over the years, this valuable life-changing message helped my three now-adult children to explore their own paths of peace and enlightened love.

Reflection of Wisdom

A mother,
a child,
the gift of enlightened love.
A time to protect them,
and then the time of freedom to fly.
Within my heart, they live.
But to themselves, they belong.

The Paintbrush

Mary Magdalene and the Sisters of the Rose

9 | T For Tau

Divine Mother Mary. She spreads her light over humanity.

The rhythm of life,
is always perfect,
it's a cycle of
unfolding events.
Everything happens
at the right time!

10
Time to Leave the Walls

Father Mother Energy

After sitting at the shrine of the Divine Mother, I was hungry and needed a walk to collect my thoughts. The weather was glorious; even the sky felt alive. On the way down to the basilica, that morning I passed a tiny authentic mom-and-pop restaurant with the delicious aroma of fresh bread and pasta. With my taste buds fired up, I knew where I was heading.

Believe me when I say I finished every mouthful of my pasta Pomodoro it was Bellissimo! Afterward, over a gelato, I sat and reflected on how much I had grown in only five days. How far I had come and, without even realizing how much I had grown over the years.

The afternoon was drawing in, and I wanted more time to visit the shrine of my beloved Saint Francis. His shrine is in the crypt at the lower level of the basilica, where his remains are interred. As I sat at the crypt with my eyes closed, I felt the presence of pure love and heard the voice of Saint Francis say, *Beloved child, for all your life, I have walked by your side. At times of pain, I have given you strength; at times of helplessness, I*

The Paintbrush

have given you hope. Your heart and love for humanity have been your greatest virtue. This dedication has helped you release your pain and that of others. You came here at this time to help remove the traumas you have experienced throughout your life; you have achieved this. Now it is time to leave the walls of Assisi and go into the countryside—to walk free; you are ready.

At that very moment, I started to cry. I thought, *What? Leave? Go outside the walls to where? Where am I going now? I don't know if I am ready!* Although I understood on a deeper level what I was being guided to do, on my human level, I wondered, *How I was supposed to leave the walls. Where was I going? Had I learned enough? What would happen if I fell back into my old ways and got lost again?*

Then I heard his voice again, *It is time to go into the countryside and leave the walls behind. Walk in faith, beloved one.* At that moment, I knew I had the choice to fall back into my old patterns or not. So, with trust in my heart and complete faith, I said, "Yes, I will go. I will listen. I am open." And just like that, I wiped my tears, pulled up my big girl panties, and walked out of the basilica.

As I stood outside the basilica, I had so much whirling around in my head. I felt such love and mothering compassion in the Divine Mother's presence. In Saint Francis' presence, I felt love and authoritarian fathering. I was tired emotionally and mentally, and my head was spinning from the message I had just heard, so I decided to take a taxi back to my hotel.

Italian Retail Therapy

On my way to the taxi rank, I walked past a store; a crocheted top caught my eye in the window. I knew my mum loved tops like that, so I decided to go inside and shop.

A few bags full of gifts later, something motivated me to ask the owner, Angelo, if there was a hotel nearby in the countryside. He said yes and took it upon himself to make the reservation for me to go there the next day.

I smile as I remember this: we were trying to communicate with one another as he repeated the hotel's name. He kept saying, "Countryside," and I would reply, "Thank you, yes, a hotel in the countryside." Finally, he went to get the phone book and showed me the name. The hotel was called the Countryside Hotel. We laughed.

I left the shop with my arms full of bags, as it was time to find a taxi. Just outside the shop was an area where taxis waited. As I walked towards one at the front of the line, it started to move forward as if to leave. So, I went to the one behind it, and as I did, the taxi driver at the front stopped and called me, "Come! Come!" In my sparse Italian, I gave him the address of the hotel I was staying at. Then I asked if he could pick me up the next day and take me to the Countryside Hotel for my next adventure. "Yes," he said in excellent English, "Of course!" So, we planned to meet the following day.

This was to be my final night within the walls of Assisi. Still, to this day, I can remember the emotion of that ending. So much love was within those walls, peace, and acceptance. Yes, I had grown, and I believed I was ready to trust. But deep down, was I?

That night under the stars, I wrote this:

The sun and the moon,
Each protects the other.
A beginning, but never an end.
As day becomes night,
night becomes day.
We are one.
Always connected.
Always together,
Heart to heart,
Never apart.
Sweet dreams, my beloved ones.
Until we meet again.
Night night.

Hermitage of Carcieri

The next morning, the taxi driver, Francesco, whom I had met the day before, arrived to pick me up. He asked me if I had visited the sacred place—the Hermitage of Carcieri—which was built around a grotto where Saint Francis used to pray. He said that the Franciscan friars still lived there in devotion to their beloved saint. And so, we drove there. Climbing, higher and higher up the mountain, way above the clouds that looked like cotton candy, and good enough to eat. I was on top of the world.

As I walked among the dwellings where Saint Francis lived, I felt as if I were stepping in his footprints. I took my shoes off and felt the energy of his presence from all those centuries ago. I envisioned how he and the friars had lived so humbly yet richly in their souls, free of bondage in their minds and hearts. I now understand more than ever what the Divine Mother was telling me about being free of needing and how we can fully embrace the gifts of peace and enlightened love by letting go of the need. Saint Francis needed nothing. All that he needed, he had. It was wonderful to be there.

Francesco said he knew I was meant to see it, and he was right; I did! As we drove down the mountain, I realized I had let go of another fear—that of heights! I leaned out of the taxi window and felt the sun on my face and the wind in my hair; I felt as free as a bird. Francesco stopped by the side of the road and picked some flowers that he then presented to me as a beautiful bouquet. Again, a total stranger I had never met before was going out of his way to bestow gifts upon me. My heart was indeed full of grace.

To the Countryside, I Go

Upon our arrival at the hotel, Francesco went inside to bring the manager to welcome me. As he introduced us, he hugged her and said to me, "Please meet the manager of the Countryside Hotel. She is a good friend of our family." Of course, he would know her—the miracles of trust and allowance were again manifesting for me right then and there! The plan was in motion when I left the basilica the day before. All of it is precise, down to the letter T!

I was shown to my room. It was beautiful, open, fresh, and inviting, but the piece de resistance was when I opened the shutters wide, my beloved Basilica of Saint Francis was in

The Paintbrush

full view. I hadn't left it. I had just gone into the countryside, outside of the walls. I cried and cried and cried. I heard, *my child, you see, I know you, your heart and soul. I know what you need! Lean on me.*

Now was my time to run in the grass of creation without a care in the world. My soul was dancing in the moonlight of my true beauty. *My soul was finally free!*

From that discovery arose this poem:

I am the sun, the sun is me,
I am the moon, the moon is me,
I am the light, and the light is me,
I am the road, and the road is me,
I am the mountain, and the mountain is me.
I am the path, and the path is me,
I am you, and you are me,
And we are one together.

As I reflect on this journey I took 18 years ago, I realize it took me 40 years to find the gift of peace and enlightened love. There is nothing more precious than that. Nothing is more alive than a feeling of belonging to everything, to the whole vast universe.

That night, as I sat in the Countryside Hotel enjoying a beautiful glass of Italian wine, I toasted to God, the Omni Presence of all that is, to the Divine Mother, Mary Magdalene, Saint Francis, and my divine self for the gifts I had received, for the guidance, the love, the belief to trust.

Reflection of Wisdom

Rejoice and sing;
a divine party is happening.
A celebration of light,
for now is your time,
walk, walk my child.
A miracle in a valley awaits you.

The Paintbrush

10 | Time to Leave the Walls

Serenity Prayer

Lord, make me an instrument of thy peace,
Where there is injury, pardon;
Where there is doubt, faith;
Where there is despair, hope;
Where there is darkness, light;
Where there is sadness, joy;
O Divine Master, grant that I may not
so much seek
To be consoled as to console,
To be understood as to understand,
To be loved as to love;
For it is in giving that we receive;
It is in pardoning that we are pardoned;
And it is in dying of the self that we are born
to eternal life.

T

11
The Paintbrush

Halo of Roses

The following day, I woke up bright and early. No longer inside the walls, I was outside in the luscious green Umbrian countryside. My heart and soul were ready for another wonderful adventure. I went downstairs for breakfast and sat near the pool under a gazebo full of flowers.

I sat for a while, enjoying my coffee, berries, and fresh-baked bread with ham and cheese. I was about to leave when someone from the hotel came to me to bring me something. On a tray, all wrapped up in a beautiful Italian cotton napkin, was a gift they told me from Francesco, the taxi driver. As they walked away, I could feel in my hands that I had been given something extraordinary.

Before opening the gift, I closed my eyes and sat with it on my lap; I just didn't want to rush this part. When I opened the napkin, inside was a halo of roses, a beautiful hand-made halo of pink roses made for me.

The Paintbrush

The note read:

Dear Tia,

The pilgrim walker of Assisi. You came here to heal yourself, and I saw you have done this through the stories you shared with me on our drive yesterday.

You inspired me to have the courage to face some of my own fears. I have been a taxi driver for many years here in Assisi and have met many people, but no one like you. My day at the basilica was ending and I was about to go home. But something made me stop, and then I saw you.

I have been brought up to believe in miracles. I think your life is now going to be full of these. This is my prayer for you. After you told me about the halo of roses the Divine Mother put on your head, driving down the mountain, I hoped maybe I could find some to pick for you.

When I got home last night, I told my wife all about your experience and the rose part, too. And so, we made this for you, child of the rose. We bless you.

Enjoy your gift from your new friends,

Francesco & Luisa.

Never had I had such a gift. The halo was made so beautifully, and I also knew the Divine Mother had an angelic hand in making this for me, too, that I knew for sure. I went into the hotel and called Francesco to thank him and his wife for the most magnificent gift anyone had ever given me. I then went upstairs to shower, change, and contemplate where to go that day. I knew I would wear my beautiful halo of roses wherever I went.

11 | The Paintbrush

Message Under a Bush

Wearing a pretty, rose-printed dress and my precious halo of roses on my braided hair, I began walking through the countryside to a special town I wanted to visit. My mind and my heart were totally at peace. And so it was that a miracle happened, just like Francesco had predicted—the miracle that was going to change my life and my family's life forever.

Walking through the countryside that day, without a care in the world, I was going with the flow. I reflected on how, being guided in silence for most of my trip, I was able to see how everything in life perfectly aligns when we let go of control and trust in the journey. There I was, walking by the sun's compass, being guided through the lush green valley on my way to the Basilica of Santa Maria Degli Angeli.

It was gorgeous and green with pockets of wildflowers growing everywhere. As I crested a small hill, out of the corner of my eye, I saw a pen lying on the ground. I remember saying, *Hmmm, I wonder why this pen is here in the middle of nowhere?* I picked it up and put it into my backpack, and carried on walking. I knew in my heart that I wasn't walking on my own; I felt that a tribe of guides was leading me every step I took. Together we were going with the flow in total serenity.

As I carried on walking, out of the corner of my eye, I noticed an old paintbrush lying under a bush—just lying there as if it was calling me to pick it up. As I bent down to pick the paintbrush up, I saw lying right next to it a lid from a bottle with the letter T on it.

The Paintbrush

T! I said to myself, *OMG. Pay attention, Tia. God is talking to you through the pen you just picked up, and now this paintbrush and the bottle lid with the T on it.*

"But why?" I said out loud, "Why did I find these things? What is the message in all of this? What am I being shown?" Why did I find that paintbrush? The pen and the bottle lid with the T on it? I sat for a while on the grass. I wanted to not rush through whatever this part was. I felt the need to be there, to just sit with my eyes closed, asking God, "Please tell me what you are showing me; what is it I need to know? I know there are no coincidences here; I feel it."

After a while, I heard this message, *be now in the moment, be flexible like a feather blowing in the wind. When the time is right, you will know more. For now, just be free to be in the awakening, allowing it to all unfold.*

What a profound message I was hearing, to be in the moment and allow myself to experience the here and now and not try to figure it all out. "I am going to listen to this message and trust," I said. "I am going to be like a feather in the wind; whatever this is all about, when the time is right, it will show itself to me."

And so, I put all my treasures in my backpack, got up, and carried on walking, feeling in my heart that they were very significant and something big and exciting was about to happen. My life was about to change, and I had no idea what that would look like. And right then, I didn't need to know.

After walking for three hours, I finally arrived at my destination, the Basilica of Santa Maria Degli Angeli. Standing outside the exquisite Italian architecture of the basilica took my breath away. It is considered the birthplace of the Order of the Friars Minor (the Franciscans).

11 | The Paintbrush

I took in the energy and beauty of this historical building that dated back to the 16th century. I especially enjoyed the rose garden and the rose chapel, where it is written that Saint Francis spent a lot of time in prayer. What a magical day I was having!

Inside the vast interior, I found the most beautiful tiny chapel called the Porziuncola chapel with exquisite frescos painted from floor to ceiling. It was one of the most magnificent, breathtaking tiny stone churches I had ever seen. This was the original church where Saint Francis first took refuge after renouncing his worldly goods. I stood in the tiny sacred space that held no more than 20 people, imagining what courage he must have had to give up his privileged life. I wondered if he had any idea of the effect he would have on the world. My heart felt so open. When you open your heart to truly living in the moment, to being present, everything in life mirrors that back to you!

Getting My Doodle On

I had always loved to doodle and draw, and finding the paintbrush inspired me to want to draw the emotions I felt rather than write about them that day. I left the basilica on a mission to find an art supply store, to buy a sketch pad, felt tips, and coloring pencils. As I wandered the streets, I noticed that the shop fronts in that area had no shop windows; they mainly looked like residential houses. Finally, I found an art supply shop, and I went inside. Looking around, I decided I needed help, so I asked an assistant if she spoke English, which she did not.

The Paintbrush

Having overheard me, a lovely lady came over to give me some assistance. With perfect English, she introduced herself. Her name was Renata. She was with her lovely 13-year-old daughter Fedora, who was a quadriplegic and unable to speak. I explained to her what I needed, and she translated this to the shop assistant for me. It's so funny when you meet an angel. You instantly feel as if you have known each other forever! Renata and Fedora were my angels that day, sent to help me on my way. Renata was so kind, and I was blessed to have met her and her daughter. After leaving the shop, we chatted outside for a little while, and then we both went on our way. I walked around the town, stopping for a coffee and pastry and to write something in my journal:

> *Knowledge.*
> *Feed your mind with the knowledge of wisdom,*
> *for within this is the secret of life.*
> *Once you begin to search within life,*
> *the truth of life begins to find you.*
> *Locked within your heart is the keeper of life.*
> *Find your key, for within the core of your being*
> *is the knowledge you yearn to unlock.*
> *Use your key wisely,*
> *for by receiving this knowledge,*
> *the blessings and the knowledge of life that you seek become yours.*

I sat for a while, taking in the deep, profound words I had written. The evening was drawing in and now it was time to make my way back to the hotel in a nice taxi ride. That evening, under the stars, I asked myself again, *why did*

11 | The Paintbrush

I find the paintbrush today? I knew there was a significance in finding it, together with the pen and the bottle top with my initial on it. I had a feeling that the paintbrush was part of the unlocking of something within my life that was yet to come. But for now, I was going to stop trying to figure it out; I was going to allow myself just to let it all unfold and trust in the process.

A Giggle Along the Way

The next morning, I woke up around 6 am. I opened the shutters and the windows then sat down to watch the sunrise, mesmerized by its beautiful colors. I knew in my heart that it was going to be another magical day. Dressed and showered by 8 am, I was ready to rock and roll! After a delicious breakfast, I hit the road running—time was of the essence as I had only two days left in Assisi to walk in the footsteps of my beloved Saint Francis. As I walked along the road, I giggled and said, "What a journey, what a life-changing journey!" Through more highs than lows, I finally met what I was looking for, and who I was looking for was *me*.

My step was much lighter; I felt freer and full of faith, strength, and trust. It was as if the road and my foot were one and the same, and my heart guided me with every step I took. What I knew for sure—this woman who originally began within those walls was not the same woman walking back that day.

I went to see Bruce and Ruth and shared with them, over a cup of tea, the story of the Countryside Hotel, the beautiful halo of roses from Francesco, the pen, the lid with a T on it

The Paintbrush

and, of course, the paintbrush lying under the bush! So many messages. I asked Bruce, "Why did I find the paintbrush?"

Bruce looked at me with a twinkle and said, "Clarity and trust, Tia!"

"Yes," I said, "clarity and trust that it will all be shown to me at the right time." And we both laughed. I was learning to be patient, letting it all unfold in its own divine time.

I said my goodbyes to Ruth and Bruce as I didn't feel I would see them again and made my way back to my beloved basilica. I stood outside its towering building with my hands on the cold stone walls. I closed my eyes and imagined myself back in time, hearing the friars talking among themselves, imagining them deep in thought with Saint Francis. I wanted to feel what it was like to be alive in his time, wondering who might have put their hand right where my hand was all those centuries ago. I had such deep gratitude and love for a place I now called home in my heart. I didn't go inside the basilica this time. I wanted to keep walking, to be in the moment, seeing all the faces and places along the way. I wanted to drink it all in and savor every moment. I was a woman walking in total serenity and trust who had arrived in search of herself but ended up finding more than she ever imagined. I was leaving complete. I was leaving whole! Every step I took, a gift had been presented to me. I no longer questioned what, when, or how. I didn't need to. I had tapped into the power of inner peace and enlightened love.

The Religion of Enlightened Love

And so, after a while, I decided to have lunch at a restaurant I hadn't been to before. Sitting down at a lovely table outside, I sat with a cold glass of local wine, toasting everyone and everything. It's truly amazing the feeling of love for no reason, just to feel alive in your heart. I was glowing; I could feel it. So much love from different experiences, so much inner peace.

And so, to express what I was feeling in a deeper way, I wrote in my journal:

> *Love is a smile, a tear, a hug, a handshake,*
> *Love is an experience—good, bad, or indifferent.*
> *Love is not perfect; love is not always kind.*
> *Love is not a false smile, the perfect weight, the perfect look.*
> *Love is in everything, and it's in everyone.*
> *Love is an experience that, come what may,*
> *Never takes your joy away.*
> *It's not a thing, a person, or a space.*
> *Love is us; love is living life!*
> *In every way, love is all of it.*

I finished my meal of fresh fish and roast potatoes, reflecting on the words I had written about love, and decided that day I would throw caution to the wind and feast like a Queen, eating whatever I fancied, calories and all. I decided I would order a cappuccino and the yummiest tiramisu I had eyed as I walked into the restaurant earlier.

While enjoying the last spoonful of my delicious dessert, out of the corner of my eye, I noticed a lovely young man. Totally out of my character, I turned to him and said, "Hello." We started chatting, and it wasn't long before he came to join me at my table. His name was Sammy, and he was from Montpelier, France. He asked me why I was in Assisi, and I shared with him some of my profound transformations and how I felt I had a calling from God to come there.

The Paintbrush

He very quickly opened to me that he had no religion, but he believed in God. I sat listening to him. After a while, I could see he was searching for something within. So, I asked him, "Do you believe in the miracle of a baby being born, puppy dogs and kittens, of seeing the rainfall, snowflakes, and the sunshine reflecting on the sea at sunset? These things you can see! Right? Well, what if that's all that you need to see? Seeing them with your heart open and through the eyes of love is all that is needed. No hate, no pain! Some see religion on one level, while others see it on another."

I said my heart believes that God is in everything, not just one religion or one place. I shared some of my experiences in Assisi—how I had learned that to me, God was in everything that exists, from every grain of sand on the beach to the sun in the sky. I told Sammy that as long as he lived with love in his heart, he was living his religion—that of enlightened love.

I sat there watching Sammy reflect on what we were sharing. Seeing someone, I didn't know suddenly feel something move within him was so wonderful. It was as if a lightbulb went off in his head and his heart! He said that was what he was searching for within himself to understand. He shared that his parents would go to church to pray, but he didn't feel in his heart that God was only in a building. He knew that God is in everything; wherever he is, God is too.

He was so excited about this revelation. And so, after we left the restaurant that afternoon, we continued our deep conversation, enjoying each other's company. He wanted to walk with me, just to hang out and chat. And so, we did. Sammy told me he was worried about his exam results and would have to wait until August to hear if he had passed. In my heart, I knew he had already passed with flying colors. A

11 | The Paintbrush

little while later, we parted ways as it was getting late and said we would stay in touch.

A few months later, I did hear from Sammy. He wrote to tell me he had passed his exams and now spent a lot of time outside in the fresh air talking to God. He wrote, "This is our special place together without walls!"

That night by the pool, as the sun was going down, I sketched the valley's landscape with the basilica in the background. What a beautiful day! I sat in reflection; so much had happened in such a short time. Minute by minute, miracle upon miracle. All of it is life changing.

That night I went to sleep with a deep sense that something beyond my wildest dreams was about to begin. I knew it had something to do with the paintbrush and that the universe knew what it was, and that was good enough for me.

The Paintbrush

Reflection of Wisdom

*A gift from God,
a passage of time,
an initiation into
a deeper awakening
that you are ready to hold.
A gift to share with the world.
Soon you will understand,
soon you will know why.*

11 | The Paintbrush

The Host of Angels. This painting invites us to see that we do not walk alone.

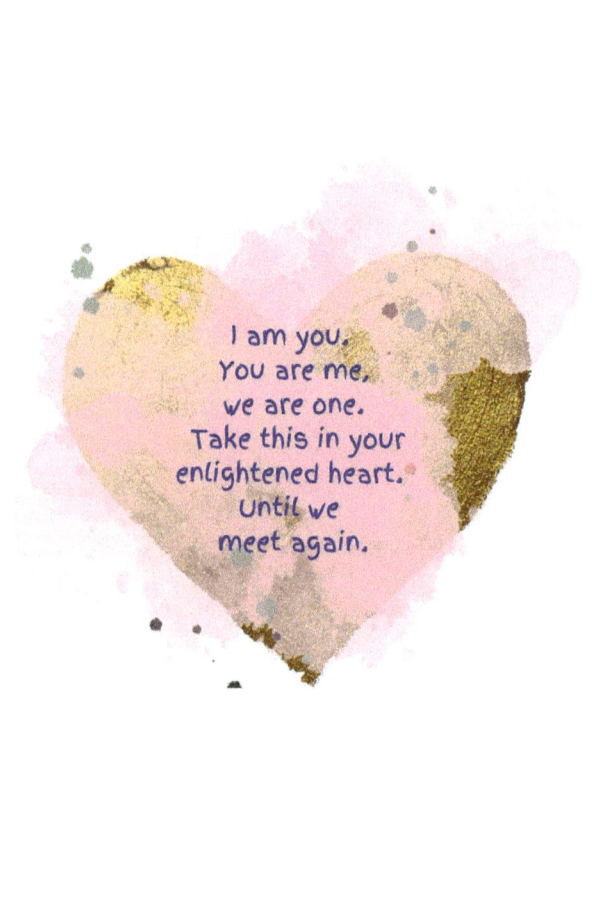

I am you.
You are me,
we are one.
Take this in your
enlightened heart.
Until we
meet again.

12
Saint Clare

At 6:30 am, I was wide awake. It was my last morning to spend some quiet time watching the sunrise. Hues of the most magnificent colors of orange and yellow lit up the morning sky. I wanted to savor every moment that I had left. I sat for a while meditating, breathing in the feeling of inner peace, and watching the clouds float by.

I decided I would create as many memories as I could that day. By 8:30 am, I was showered, dressed, and ready to get going. After having a lovely breakfast, I made my way back into town, this time to visit the Basilica of Saint Clare.

As I walked that day, I noticed how clean the streets were for the first time. No trash or litter anywhere. Except for bird feathers, loads of feathers. I picked a few up and a penny that I found next to them. Pennies to me are a gift from my Nana Lily, reminding me that she is always with me. As I carried on walking, I said to myself, *A penny for your thoughts today, Tia. It's an amazing feeling to be alive in the world today!*

As I held the feather in my hand, I imagined that it was a magic wand and as I walked, I waved it in the air! I wanted to spread my joy everywhere.

The Paintbrush

Alive With Light

Walking into Saint Clare's Basilica, I felt the presence of feminine innocence. It was much softer than the fathering presence I felt in Saint Francis' Basilica. Her story is similar to Saint Francis's. Both were born into tremendous wealth to powerful parents living in Umbria. Both wanted to help the poor and dedicated their lives to that.

Saint Clare of Assisi was born around July 16th, 1194. Members of her household knew her to be a sensitive child, prayerful and kind. From a young age, Clare wanted to help the poor, even though she lived a very privileged life; in fact, living a wealthy life made her quite unhappy. Her mother, a devout Catholic, taught Clare and her siblings from a very young age all about the teachings of Jesus. With no desire to marry at 18, the young Clare ran away from her father's home. Along the road that night, she met some Franciscan friars carrying torches and joined them as they walked to a poor little chapel called the Portiuncula. There, Clare exchanged her rich clothing for common cloth and her bejeweled belt for one made of rope with knots. And it was there also that she sacrificed her long, beautiful hair that Saint Francis himself cut off.

While living in a Benedictine convent, one day, her father and uncles stormed into the chapel, intending to take her home in a fit of rage. Clare, clinging to the church's altar, threw off her veil to show her father her cropped hair, remaining adamant that she was not leaving.

Sixteen days later, her sister Agnes joined her, too. Together with other women, they lived a simple life of great poverty, deep service to humanity, and were completely

12 | Saint Clare

secluded from the world. Together Saint Francis and Saint Clare founded The Poor Clares, officially known today as the Order of Saint Clare.

In 1216 at the age of 21, Francis ordained Clare to accept the office of abbess, which she kept until her death. Clare herself never left the chapel walls of San Damiano. During her time as the abbess (Mother Superior), Clare dedicated much of her time to changing the governing rules of the order from the old Benedictine ways to the newly established Franciscan rulings.

Two days before Clare died, Pope Innocent IV finally approved her order. Saint Clare is buried in the crypt in the basilica where people from far and wide visit just to sit at her shrine. Some come to ask for healing, some come for a miracle, and some come just to be there.

Sitting in the crypt that morning, with my eyes closed, I felt a deep presence of love and serenity in the air. At this basilica, the nuns of Saint Clare make the most wonderful candles. I remember buying many to take home with me—so many that months after leaving Assisi, every time I lit one, I would feel the power of peace around me, as if I were right back there with Saint Clare. It's funny how just by sharing this with you so many years later, I can truly feel and see one of those candles lit up and glowing with love in my mind's eye.

Just for a moment, let's see that together. Imagine right now that we—you and I—are looking at one of those sacred candles glowing ever so bright. The flame is tall and strong, flickering bigger and brighter, getting stronger and stronger as it reflects the energy of omnipresent love. Imagine the flame is full of wishes—wishes for peace and healing for our world,

The Paintbrush

full of unconditional, enlightened love and kindness for all mankind. Just keep seeing this in your heart. See it as the power of prayer creating miracles in the here and now. Today, just in this small but powerful way, I see we are creating this together.

In my heart, as I was sitting in the crypt, I felt such a deep connection to Saint Clare. I understood the courage it takes to be different. As you have read, I had gone to Assisi believing I was lost, but I was not. I learned that I had always walked with courage, that being true to yourself means not conforming to please others, and that that takes strength. What a wonderful way to finish my journey—meeting Saint Clare on my final day; I felt complete.

I was leaving with so much wisdom and a deeper knowing of truth in my heart. I understood that love for myself, nourishing me, and living my authentic truth was how I would keep my empathic shield strong and empowered. What a perfect way to finish. More than ever, my heart was full of the power of enlightened love, inner strength, and purpose.

As I started to leave the basilica, I passed by two nuns smiling with so much joy in their eyes. Their total devotion said it all. I could feel the warmth of their hearts and their love for their beloved patron Saint Clare. Love, it is. It's all about enlightened love.

I left the basilica and blew a kiss into the air, feeling so much gratitude for such a transformational journey. I felt humbled that I had been guided to go on this life-changing adventure.

Outside I found an area to sit down. The sun was warm and inviting; I had this feeling that I needed to write, to share from my heart some words, and so, sitting with my back against an old wall, I wrote in my journal this:

*I walk in faith for now I see,
that we are all part of humanity.
The good, the bad, the happy, the sad,
Rich or poor,
All are part of each other.
No judgment, no shame, no blame.
For now, I see with truth and love
life is like a beautiful flame,
shining bright, illuminating the way,
and leading us to embrace
the moments we have each and every day.
For we are all winners in this game called Life,
even through our sorrows and strife.
For now, I see clearly all that we need comes from within.
And now it is time for me to return home
and to let it all begin.*

In releasing myself from the chains of illusion, I found the part of myself I had been searching for all my life. In letting go of what no longer served me, I found a deeper presence of God within me—the omnipresence of divine beauty, truth, love, and oneness. I was no longer empty. My vessel was full, overflowing with inner peace and enlightened love.

My Panties and Me

I was returning home lighter in my heart, mind, body, and soul! Oh, and definitely in my luggage, too.

The Paintbrush

The night before, I had met a lovely lady sitting on the side of the road, as I was walking into my hotel. I asked her if she needed anything. She told me how she helped women and children in need in her broken English! "Perfect," I said, "I have so much to give away," so we planned to meet the next evening so I could give her all my clothes.

With not much to pack, I decided to go and treat myself to something yummy for lunch. I walked away from the basilica with a spring in my foot. Suddenly, I saw Renata and Fedora right in front of me—the mother and daughter, my new friends that I had met at the art supply store. Renata treated me as if I were her long-lost friend. We hugged and kissed and chatted for a while.

It's amazing, isn't it—*miracles do happen!* And to this day, they have not stopped.

A year after I left Assisi, Jonathan and I went to Venice to visit Renata and her daughter in their hometown, and we spent a few days getting to know her and her family.

Once you open yourself up to living life in faith and wonderment, miracles become a natural way of life.

And so, I kissed them goodbye that day outside Saint Clare's Basilica and made my way to a lovely café where I ordered the most delicious fresh margarita pizza with fresh pesto and roasted garlic. Not only was I stretching time, but I was also stretching my waistband too!

Love From Us All

And so, it was time to make my way back to the basilica to say goodbye to my beloved Saint Francis. I stood in front of his crypt, with a bursting sense of love pouring out of me.

Although I was sad to leave, I felt a powerful sense of peace within. I heard his voice say to me, *you will never leave, my child. You see, even in the countryside, you did not leave us. You are taking us with you in your heart. There is nothing in these walls—walls are walls. It's all within your heart; everything else is all an illusion. For we are in everything that shines love. It is time, my child, to go into the world and share your light, to be the vision of compassion and love, and make your voice heard. Remember what the Divine Mother said, I am you, and you are me, and we are one together. Always. This is a reflection of us all as one.*

And so it was that I left my beloved ones—the Divine Mother, Saint Francis, Saint Mary Magdalene, and Saint Clare —with a full heart.

Artist of Assisi

As I walked back to the hotel, I passed by a beautiful art gallery. I walked inside and looked around. The art was vibrant, colorful, and alive. The artist had completely captured the essence of the love I felt in Assisi through his choice of colors.

I stood mesmerized in front of the painting of Jesus alive on the cross when a man walked up to me with a glass of wine in his hand. I turned, saw a charismatic smile, and heard his beautiful Italian voice say, "Hi, I'm Raffaele Ariante. I am the artist. Would you care for a glass of wine?"

Beaming with pride, he walked me around his gallery. He told me about each painting and its spiritual meanings. I was especially captured by one painting of a house with a beautiful sun above it. It represented the basilica in Assisi

The Paintbrush

and the balance of the sun and moon. There was a bird on the roofline that represented being your higher self without chains of judgment. In the middle, I saw a palette of color representing my ability to paint life the way I saw it. The flower that stood on its own was blooming with the enlightened love of knowing who it truly was. I decided to buy a few art pieces from Raffaele to take home for friends and family.

We chatted for a while about Saint Francis and how I had been drawn to come to Assisi. I shared with him about the paintbrush I found lying under a bush. He jokingly said that maybe finding the paintbrush was a sign that I was to become his art ambassador in London to sell his art. I remember smiling and saying to him, "That is a wonderful idea. Maybe you are right. We will just have to wait and see."

And so, it was time to say farewell to the walls of my beloved Assisi. "Thank you for it all," I said. I felt as if I had traveled through time, through centuries of past lives that I had lived, lost, and now found again in this lifetime. One thing I knew for sure—my heart would always be here in Assisi, and one day I would return to tell a new story.

And so, I made my way back to the hotel, where right on time, the lovely lady I had met the day before sitting outside my hotel was waiting with her granddaughter to collect my clothes. I carefully folded the clothes and placed them in a basket I had purchased in town just for this. What a feeling of gratitude I felt in giving them to her! I might not have started my journey with just my panties. But I was for sure leaving with just them. Lighter and brighter.

That night under the beautiful evening sky with my halo of roses on my head, I toasted to a journey that will stay in my heart forever. I toasted to all the life experiences that had brought me to Assisi. I toasted to courage, strength, virtue, beauty, self-love, and all the broken pieces that were now whole.

With just a small overnight bag to pack with the gifts I had bought, a couple of outfits, and my panties, I spent a little while before bed writing these words:

> *We are the drivers on this road called life,*
> *Some take shortcuts,*
> *Some take the long road home,*
> *Some drive fast, some drive slow.*
> *Some are in a hurry; some go with the flow.*
> *One thing's for sure; we get there in the end.*
> *Happy cruising this road called life.*

In my heart tomorrow, I was taking the perfect road home.

The Paintbrush

Until We Meet Again

And so it was that my journey in Assisi was over and inner peace and enlightened love were what I was taking home with me in my heart. It was the final morning, and I was up before the sun rose as my next destination was Lucca. It was there that I was to meet Jonathan. You see, he had called me a few days earlier to tell me that I was very missed and that even the dog had gone on strike! He was flying to Italy to bring me home.

Lucca was quite a long drive from Assisi. Guess who was taking me there. Yes, you are right, my dear friend Francesco. As I sat in Francesco's car, looking back at the hotel and the Basilica of Saint Francis in the distance, I remembered the woman who seven days earlier looked back at her house on her way to Italy. I was now returning as the embodiment of enlightened love. I was on a mission, ready to share her with my husband, children, and the world. I was ready, and my beloved ones in Assisi knew I was, too.

Driving through the countryside, Francesco stopped every so often to pick me flowers. This time he had brought me a vase. "You must put this vase in your room at the hotel," he said, smiling. "You see," as he handed me the wildflowers, "these are the flowers of the goddess of passion. When she was returned once more to her beloved, God sent a host of angels with bountiful gifts. This is your time to receive these gifts," he said. With a kind smile, he added, "You deserve this and so much more, Tia, Love!"

Life was waiting for me and in Lucca, so was Jonathan.

Reflection of Wisdom

Rejoice, rejoice,
the mountain she climbed,
the sun has risen,
it is her time to shine!

The Paintbrush

Saint Clare and Her Devout Sisters

12 | Saint Clare

The Eye of Knowledge and Wisdom

13
Birthing My Art

Ahhhh…I hear you asking, "But what about the paintbrush you found that day? Did you ever discover the meaning behind it?"

Well, of course, I did!

As soon as I returned from Assisi, I called Marisol. I was so excited to share all my adventures with her, especially the one about finding the paintbrush and the lid that was lying next to it. Although we hadn't seen each other in more than six months, it was as if our time apart had never happened. She quickly came over and we picked up right where we left off. We both agreed that the paintbrush and the bottle cap with the letter T on it was a message from God, and at some point, I would know what it all meant!

I remember reflecting on my reunion with my darling Marisol. What a journey. Had we not gone our own separate ways, had I not gone on a journey on my own to learn something new, none of this deep transformation would have happened. God knows! It's all in divine timing. That night I went to bed with deep trust in my heart with the lid and the paintbrush by my bed as a reminder that I now lived in pure faith.

The Paintbrush

So it happened, three months later. One day, Marisol called to tell me she had a client who needed nine unusual paintings made.

"Great, Marisol! I know who could do this, my friend Raffaele Ariante, the artist I met in Assisi." I replied.

Unbeknownst to me, she had another plan. Can you guess what it was? After a long, silent pause, she said, "Tia!"

"Yes Mari," I replied.

"You're painting them. That is why you found the paintbrush and the bottle cap with the T on it."

I went into total silence, and all I could think of was, *No, No, No, No!*

I asked her if she was drinking. Then my next reaction was to say, "I can't. I don't know how to paint! What happens if I get it wrong? I don't know what I'm doing!" At that moment, I jumped right back into my old programming.

But Marisol wasn't taking no for an answer. "I know you can do it, Tia, I believe in you, and by the sounds of it, God believes in you, too. I watched how you shared your story with me with so much joy, especially the part about the paintbrush, the lid from a bottle, and the pen. I know this is a sign; just like Moses found God at the burning bush, you found God at your bush, too. The paintbrush and the bottle lid are bringing you a message."

I paused, thinking about the profound message she had just shared with me. She was right! So, I took a deep breath and said, "I will do it."

As her clients wanted unusually looking art made with leather, metal, and paint, Marisol and I went a few days later to a hardware store to find pieces I could use for the painting. I remember that day as if it was yesterday. With a bag of grommets and nails, pots of white, silver, and gold paint, and nine three-foot canvases, I was ready to make her clients the room divider screen they wanted made from art.

Before I started to paint, I closed my eyes, lit one of my Saint Clare candles, and asked my beloved guides to come into my hands and help me paint the energy of light and enlightened love. I called on the Divine Mother, Saint Francis, Saint Clare, and Mary Magdalene—to please be with me.

The minute I started to paint, I felt something within me was on fire with passion and purpose. I had this knowing, this awareness that I knew what to do; I could feel it coming from within me. The presence of light was guiding my hand. I was so inspired that I completed all the paintings within a week.

My heart felt so much love for these pieces. I would stand in awe of them every day. I would be mesmerized by their presence as if they were alive with energy, not just pieces of art on a canvas but portals of light beyond this world.

When I called Marisol to tell her they were finished, she was shocked! "Finished? How? When? I'm coming over!"

Finished and fabulous they were. We danced around the house together with so much happiness in our souls. My heart had birthed my art.

I remember the day we installed the paintings, the lady of the house, Marisol's client, came up to me and said, "Your gift is from God; through your hands, your heart speaks. I feel the world needs to hear your voice." I will never forget those words. As I left the house that afternoon, I remember sitting

The Paintbrush

in the car with tears of love as I thanked the Divine Mother for helping me make my voice be heard through art. Every step I had taken in life was all planned; nothing was by chance. When we show up completely, aligning with that bigger part of our conscious awareness, we draw in our enlightened self. It was time to live this more than ever, I felt it in my heart, and as I left the clients home, I blew a kiss into the air to all my beloved guides and said, "A new adventure begins. Let's do it."

That was in 2004. That was the part that was waiting to be awakened within me. And so an artist was born! In 2012 at one of the world's largest art exhibitions in Manhattan, I exhibited my artwork and won an award for being one of the top ten artists at the show. Today my art hangs in public places, private homes, hospitals, and palaces worldwide.

And so, my darling friends, if I can change my life, I promise you, with all my heart and soul, so can you. This is why I wrote my story—to inspire you to live your life enthusiastically, to give yourself permission to dance outside of the line and live this miracle called life. I promise you with all my heart, it will be worth it.

And so, I will finish as I begin!

What if all you needed every day was a paintbrush, some paint, and the world as your canvas in order to create your life the way you want it to be?

Until we meet again on this road called life.
Your friend and traveling companion,
Tia Crystal

Reflection of Wisdom

Take that leap of faith.
Let passion be your guide.
Step out of your comfort zone.
Travel light.
Be brave.
Be bold.
Dance into life.
You have nothing to lose
and everything to gain.

The Paintbrush

This was one of my first paintings. It is of my guide White Cloud and hangs in my private collection.

An Inspiring Message from Tia's Children

Dear Mum,

Reading through this book has inspired us. We are so glad you can finally share this part of your story with the world because the world needs to read this.

You inspire us to be the best versions of ourselves and always to follow our dreams every day, to listen to our inner voice and trust our intuition, to live with happiness in our hearts, and always have a smile on our faces, just like you.

We feel so blessed to be your children as we watch you on your journey to making a difference in the world. We are so excited for you, Mum, and look forward to seeing how the next chapter of your life unfolds. It's so rewarding to witness how far you have come, as we know your journey has not always been easy for you, especially with your early learning challenges with dyslexia. Even through your highs and lows, you have always had a beautiful aura of love and have never lost that. It seems like you have already lived a thousand lives, and now you are starting a new adventure again.

The Paintbrush

Thank you for everything you do, not just for us, but for everyone you meet and the lives you change daily.

Love you always,
Your children, Melissa, James, and Joshua

This painting is called *Enlightened One*.
It represents the beauty of being a pillar of light
and shining bright.

The Paintbrush

About the Author

Tia Crystal is an award-winning artist, masterful storyteller, public speaker, best-selling author, and humanitarian. Dedicated to spreading light in the world, Tia inspires the soul's energy to awaken to the possibilities that lie within. You can feel the hand of creation through everything she touches. Her art contains crystals, gemstones, and other minerals that emanate light for the viewers' awakening.

She is a woman on a mission to sprinkle magic and joy into the world. On her exclusive retreats, Tia facilitates personal growth that inspires you to find your creativity as a way of navigating life.

Tia, her three grown children, Melissa, James, and Joshua, and two grand puppies, Gatsby the Sheepadoodle and Rennie the Bernedoodle, are blessed to call the USA their home. She loves family retreats, hanging out with friends, baking layered fondant iced cakes, sailing the Mediterranean, and reading under an umbrella at the beach on a glorious sunny day.

The Paintbrush

Award-Winning Artist

Eighteen years after her life-changing trip to Assisi and finding her paintbrush, today Tia Crystal is a sought-after artist. She has channeled her creativity into many unique artistic masterpieces for nearly two decades. Each one is encrusted in crystals, is alive with lifeforce, and has its unique presence.

In 2008, Tia opened the Healing Art Gallery, in the heart of downtown Boca Raton. Her philanthropic nature led her to affiliate with the Florence Fuller Center (fullercenterfl.org), the Children's Unicorn Foundation (unicornchildrensfoundation.org), and the Children's Museum, where every week, children enjoyed Storytime with Miss Tia as she brought whimsical stories alive in their imagination.

In 2012, Tia was formally recognized as one of the Top ten Artists at the Javits Center Art Exhibition, the world's largest fine-art show in Manhattan, New York, only eight years after putting her paintbrush to canvas.

In 2016, her artistic expression transferred into jewelry when Tia launched the Luv Tia Jewelry Collection on QVC, the television shopping network.

In 2020 her art was featured at the Art in Wellness exhibition at the United Nations in Geneva, Switzerland.

Several pieces of artwork (some are featured in this book) are available at the beautiful Gaia Contemporary Art on Canyon Road in Santa Fe, New Mexico.

Today her commissioned masterpieces are collector's items. Tia's paintings have been commissioned by well-known celebrities and are on display worldwide. They hang

13 | About the Author

in galleries, resorts, and private residences around the world, including a palace in Dubai.

"Light pours through me as I work," Tia says. "I believe the jewels that are buried within us are reflected on the canvases I create." When you shine a light on her paintings, you can see the energy moving through them. Tia understands that her art is an organic life force, a deeper expression of the divine. Viewing her work is an invitation to enliven your own light and bring it out into the world.

Tia's intricate creations can take up to 6 months to create. She takes time to connect with your energy and the energy of light and enlightened love so that when she's finished, and the art is hanging in your home, you experience this each and every day. To commission Tia for one of her masterpieces, contact Tia@TiaCrystal.com.

The Paintbrush

Masterful Storyteller

In 2020 to help children stay connected to wonderment and joy, Tia launched E Me Uni®, a media company that teaches children that their uniqueness is their gift. They are perfect just the way they are. The main character, a magical, enchanting unicorn called E Me Uni® was born out of Tia's enlightened heart. He inspires children to believe in the magic in themselves and to know that they have the ability to create anything they desire. By keeping their imagination alive through storytelling, Miss Tia and E Me Uni teach children how to tap into their uniqueness through character building, mindfulness, mental/spiritual literacy, and play, transforming their doubts and fears into endless possibilities.

Tia's vision is for every child to learn that it is great to be who you are and it's time to shine. Her goal is to remind children to share positivity daily, be mindful of their thoughts, and find positive solutions to everyday issues. Tia and her team are dedicated to impacting children and families across the globe through E Me Uni®.

Imagination is everything. It is the preview of life's coming attractions. – Albert Einstein

Welcome to the magical world of E Me Uni®
Website: emeuni.com
YouTube channel: E Me Uni
Instagram : instagram.com/uni_luvs/
Facebook: facebook.com/UniLuvs

Public Speaker

In 2018, Tia formed B Wellness Travel Retreats, and Be Wellness Mind creating leadership and enrichment programs around the globe for corporate presidents and C-level executives.

In 2022 Tia was invited to be a speaker along with Katie Ford from the Ford Foundation and other powerful women at a gathering of over 100 people for International Women's Day. Tia will be a featured speaker at this event in 2023, talking about the woman behind the story of *The Paintbrush*.

Tia is available for corporate training and keynote presentations.

Best-Selling Author

Her next two books, *The Artist Awakens* and *Enlightened Love* are coming soon!

Tia is dedicated to keeping the art of imagination alive and building a movement that inspires the world and the next generation of children to be kind, caring, and accepting of each other's differences.

Through her art, her heart, and her storytelling, she makes this dream come true.

Welcome to Tia's world of imagination where anything and everything is possible.

Contact Tia Crystal

TiaCrystal.com
ThePaintbrush@TiaCrystal.com
Intuitive Mindspace work: bewellnessmind.com
Exclusive Retreats: bwellnesstravel.com
E Me Uni: emeuni.com

The Paintbrush

Knowledge & Wisdom. Buried deep within us is the knowledge and the wisdom of our ancestors who came before. If only walls could talk! This piece hangs in the Gaia Contemporary Gallery in Santa Fe, New Mexico.

Lumiere—light. This painting transports you into a different dimension of light. In the eyes of the beholder, it brings you into a deeper place of peace. This piece hangs in the Gaia Contemporary Gallery in Santa Fe, New Mexico.

www.ingramcontent.com/pod-product-compliance
Lightning Source LLC
LaVergne TN
LVHW051040070526
838201LV00067B/4876